*Here's what the reviewers are saying about*
# The Entrepreneur's Road Map
## to Business Success –

"...the book is well-written. Its easy-to-read format with highlighted key ideas and 'Summary Tours' at the end of every chapter all but give the reader the capital to get started."
**Mark Agusti**
*The Beach Reporter*

"The advice is good, the examples, suggestions profuse, the important points are in bold print for easy reference... Not only is this an advisor for business but it also offers suggestions for positive thinking." ***The Book Reader***

"*The Entrepreneur's Road Map* will guide a creative person with a dream towards success by providing them with sound and fundamental business principles."
**Steve Lewis**
**Lewis Micro Systems, Inc.**

## About the Authors –

*Lyle Maul,* at the age of 35, retired from one company he cofounded that had achieved annual sales in excess of $300 million by its sixth full year.

*Dianne Mayfield,* a lawyer who believes it is never too late to follow your heart and pursue your dreams, began her entrepreneurial adventures at the age of 35.

*Now Both* serve as consultants, advisors and occasional investors to other entrepreneurs through their consulting firm, **VENTURE SERVICES GROUP.**

**Lyle Maul and Dianne Mayfield**
**Coauthors of**
*The Entrepreneur's Road Map*
*to Business Success*

# The Entrepreneur's Road Map

## To
## Business Success

By

*Lyle R. Maul, M.B.A.*
and
*Dianne Craig Mayfield, J.D.*

Cover Design by
**D-SQUARED**

Published by

*Saxtons River Publications*
*P.O. Box 1609*
*Alexandria, Virginia  22313*

THE ENTREPRENEUR'S ROAD MAP

*Cover Design by*:  **D-SQUARED**

**Library of Congress Cataloging in Publication Data:**

Maul, Lyle R.
    The entrepreneur's road map to business success / by Lyle R. Maul,
Dianne C. Mayfield
    Spine title: The Entrepreneur's road map.

    Includes index.
    1. New business enterprises.    2. Entrepreneurship.    3. Success in
business.

I. Mayfield, Dianne C.  II. Title.  III. Title: Entrepreneur's road map.
HD62.5.M37    1990            658.4'21--dc20            88-61260
ISBN 0-929382-06-4

BOMC offers recordings and compact discs, cassettes
and records. For information and catalog write to
BOMR, Camp Hill, PA 17012.

*Dedicated to*
*every person who dares to*
*embark on an entrepreneurial journey.*

# Table of Contents

Acknowledgements

## An Introduction To The Entrepreneur's Road Map

1

The Natural Thing to Do                    2
Entrepreneur v. Intrapreneur               3
About the Authors                          4
Road Map Format                            6
Enjoy the Journey!                         7
**Summary Tour**                           8


## Chapter 1
## The Entrepreneurial Traveler
### A PROFILE OF THE ENTREPRENEUR

9

The Meaning of "Entrepreneur"              9
Belief in the Idea and in Yourself        11
Simplicity/Big-Picture Orientation        15
Creativity                                16
Flexible Planning                         18
Optimism                                  20
Realism                                   21
Communication                            22
Risk-Taking                              24
Persistence                              26
Action-Orientation                       28
**Summary Tour**                          29

*Chapter 2*
## *Choosing Your Destination*                          33
### SELECTING A BUSINESS IDEA

The Basics                                              33
Discovering Business Ideas                              37
Analyzing the Options                                   43
    Time Considerations                   47
    Financing                             50
    Level of Expertise                    52
    Risk Comfort-Level                    53
    Financial Return                      54
Alternatives to Creating a Business
  "From Scratch"                                 58
    Licensing                             58
    Franchises/Distributorships           60
    Acquiring an Existing Business        62
    Becoming an Intrapreneur              63
  Travel Partners                              65
  **Summary Tour**                             68

*Chapter 3*
## *Planning Your Itinerary*                            71
### THE BUSINESS PLAN

Purpose of the Business Plan                            71
Preparation and Presentation of the
    Business Plan                         77
**Summary Tour**                                        85

*Chapter 4*
## *Designing the Tour Package*                         87
### MARKETING STRATEGIES

Marketing Philosophy and Strategy   *87*

Selecting the Target Market   *92*

Creating the Image   *97*

   Value of the Product   *99*

   Name, Logo and Slogan   *102*

      Descriptive Names   *103*

      Coined Descriptive Names   *104*

      Symbolic Names   *105*

      Founder Names   *105*

      "Off the Wall" Names   *106*

      Nebulous Names   *108*

      Protecting Names, Logos and
         Slogans   *108*

   Physical Appearance   *109*

   Location   *113*

Pricing   *114*

Promoting the Product   *119*

**Summary Tour**   *123*

*Chapter 5*
# *Financing the Expedition*
## FINANCING THE BUSINESS

*127*

Financing Strategies   *127*

   Multiple Sources   *129*

   Presentation Hints   *131*

   Good Marketer   *133*

   Positive Attitude   *135*

   New v. Tried Concept   *138*

   Amount and Type of Financing   *139*

   Selection Criteria   *143*

   Ongoing Relations With Your Investors   *144*

Financing Phases   *145*

Financing Sources                                     147
   Personal Funds                               148
   Family and Friends                           149
   Private Investors                            150
   Banks                                        151
   Factoring                                    155
   Venture Capitalists                          155
   Investment Bankers                           158
   Public Offering                              159
   Franchising                                  161
   Corporate Sponsors                           162
   State and Federal Government Sources          164
   Customer Financing                           164
   Grants                                       165
   Foreign Resources                            166
   Additional Financing Alternatives for
     an Ongoing Business                 167
Structuring the Deal                                  167
Timing of Additional Financing for an
   Ongoing Business                             173
Using Finders or Brokers                              176
**Summary Tour**                                      178

*Chapter 6*
*Moving on Down the Road*                             183
**SALES AND DISTRIBUTION**

Distinction Between Sales and Marketing               183
Distribution Channels                                 185
Getting the Best Sales Mileage                        195
Sales Slumps                                          199
**Summary Tour**                                      201

*Chapter 7*
## *Staying on Course*     *203*
### MANAGING THE BUSINESS

| | |
|---|---|
| Meaning of Management | *203* |
| Qualities of Successful Managers/Leaders | *204* |
|     Sound Business Judgment | *205* |
|     Self-Confidence | *206* |
|     Consistency | *206* |
|     Communication Skills | *207* |
|     Respect and Support for Employees | *208* |
|     Creating an Atmosphere of Teamwork | *209* |
|     Leading by Example | *210* |
|     Understanding Personal Strengths and | |
|        Weaknesses | *211* |
| Management Techniques | *211* |
|     Keep It Simple | *212* |
|     Management by Objective | *213* |
|     Management by Exception | *214* |
|     Management by Motivation | *215* |
|     Reviewing and Revising Management | |
|        Goals | *217* |
|     Selecting the Management Team | *217* |
| Agreements With Key Employees | *221* |
| **Summary Tour** | *222* |

*Chapter 8*
## *Tour Guides*     *225*
### WORKING WITH BUSINESS ADVISORS

| | |
|---|---|
| Selecting Business Advisors | *225* |
| Working With Business Advisors | *230* |
| **Summary Tour** | *234* |

*Chapter 9*
## Avoiding Detours
237
### ANTICIPATING AND AVOIDING OBSTACLES

Imagined v. Real Success                237
   Industry Comparisons                240
   Cash Reserves                        240
   Sales Base                           240
   Profits                              241
   Response of Financiers               242
   Business Plan Goals                  245
   Entrepreneur's Goals                 245
Strengthen the Core Business            246
Potential Temptations                   248
   Business Diversification             250
   Outside Temptations                  253
The Big Reward                          255
**Summary Tour**                        257

*Chapter 10*
## Conclusion
259

*Appendix A* — *The Entrepreneur's Business*
                  *Start-up Checklist*        265

*Appendix B* — *Sample Outline of a Business Plan*   293

*Appendix C* — *Resources*               297

*Glossary of Financial Terms*            303

*Index*                                  315

# Acknowledgements

The authors wish to express their gratitude to the following people for their assistance, ideas and other support in developing this book: Cory Amron, Melinda Barnett, Kitty Barrett, Andrea Bridgeman, Deborah Caulfield, Anne-Marie Cooney, Ferricia Harris, Marsha Greenfield, Phil Jones, Steve Lewis, Sandra Phelps, Janet Smith and Josie Zainhofsky.

Special thanks are extended to Charlene Craig, Linda Maul and Nancy Ryback for their significant contributions toward the completion of this project.

# Acknowledgments

The authors wish to express their gratitude to the following people for their guidance, ideas and other assistance in preparing this book: [illegible names] ...

Special thanks are extended to [illegible] for their continuation toward the completion of this project.

# An Introduction To
# The Entrepreneur's Road Map

*Entrepreneur* – the word evokes images of the adventurer, the pioneer, an independent spirit in pursuit of the fulfillment of passions and dreams, one who dares assume the risk of the success or failure of a business venture. The entrepreneur's journey from the starting point of an idea to the destination of a successful business is a long one, filled with crossroads, detours, and unexpected challenges.

This book for entrepreneurs by entrepreneurs is designed as a road map – a guide to the most direct route from the idea stage to the operational business. From firsthand experience, the authors map strategies for anticipating and avoiding potential road hazards, choosing the best option at forks in the road, and enjoying the journey more by seeing the road more clearly.

This road map is written not only for the traveler who has never embarked on an entrepreneur's journey, but also for the experienced explorer who understands and appreciates the value of a road map for guiding present and future journeys.

## *The Natural Thing to Do*

❖ **Being an entrepreneur is the natural thing to do.**

Being an entrepreneur is the natural thing to do. From the earliest days of civilization, as we know it, entrepreneurs have been building businesses. Long before the days of corporate conglomerates, there were merchants, shopkeepers, farmers, fishermen, and countless other tradesmen who ventured to form their own businesses. Almost all of today's corporate giants were at one time entrepreneurial startups. American business was built by entrepreneurs and continues to grow because of new entrepreneurs.

Following the entrepreneur's path is a natural choice on life's journey. The essence of life is creativity and growth. Every living organism – from the single cell to advanced life forms, such as the human being – possesses the innate drive to create and to grow. Likewise, the essence of being an entrepreneur is to create and grow – businesses.

Successful entrepreneurs do not have a stereotypical profile. People of every age, race, sex, background and management style have created successful businesses. Sometimes the entrepreneurial drive is evident in a person from childhood. For instance, the creator of Lionel trains built his first train at the age of seven, tinkered with gadgets throughout his boyhood, and launched his manufacturing company at the age of twenty-three. Other times the drive is born suddenly because of something that occurs in the person's day-to-day life or business career – perhaps disillusionment with an employment position ignites a burning desire to start a business; or perhaps an annoying problem sparks a quest for a creative solution, which leads to the invention of a new product or service.

If you have that creative, entrepreneurial drive in your soul, why just watch someone else reap the psychological and monetary benefits of starting a business when you could be starting one yourself?

Of course, the decision to start a business should not be made blindly. The chosen business should be one that has real market potential and the founder should clearly understand both the potential upsides and downsides of the endeavor before jumping into it. This road map provides guidance for deciding whether or not to proceed on the path of the entrepreneur, assessing the viability of various business options, and successfully converting your chosen goal into a reality.

## *Entrepreneur v. Intrapreneur*

❖ **If you have the drive to create, find an outlet for it, whether within your own business or within the business of another.**

There are many who have felt the entrepreneurial drive but have chosen not to express it. Perhaps the timing is inappropriate for assuming risks due to financial, family, or other obligations; or perhaps the drive is there, but the idea that would justify "taking the plunge" has not surfaced.

A fortunate alternative has emerged, which appropriately has been dubbed the "intrapreneur." The intrapreneur is the person who possesses the qualities of an entrepreneur, but who expresses them while remaining an employee within someone else's company or organization.

Companies that have recognized and promoted the intrapreneur have created a "win/win" situation, benefiting both the company and the employee. The company benefits by retaining a creative employee and profiting from that person's ideas. The employee benefits by having an outlet for creative expression and increased financial reward without excessive financial risk.

This road map is written for the intrapreneur, as well as for the entrepreneur. The underlying message for both is: If you have the drive to create, find an outlet for it, whether within your own business or within the business of another. For the most part, the same principles apply in both settings. The primary difference is that the potential risks and rewards are usually lower for the intrapreneur than for the entrepreneur.

## About The Authors

The authors are seasoned entrepreneurial travelers. They have experienced and observed, firsthand, both the successes and failures of companies in a wide variety of industries. These experiences have provided valuable insights into certain key principles that have led to successful business endeavors, as well as guidelines for avoiding hazards and detours along the way. Through this road map, they share these key principles and guidelines with other travelers.

Lyle Maul has been a principal investor, co-founder, and/or key executive in over a dozen start-up businesses in a variety of different industries, including microcomputer, real estate, health care, mail-order, restaurant, clothing-accessory, and publishing companies. One successful company that he co-founded achieved an annual sales volume in excess of $100 million in its fourth full year of business, $200 million in its fifth year and will exceed $300 million in its sixth full year of operation. According to *Inc.* Magazine, this company was the fifth fastest-growing, privately-held company in the nation in 1988.

Lyle began building businesses in his early twenties, while earning a Bachelor's Degree in Business Administration and a Master's Degree in Entrepreneurship and Venture Management from the University of Southern California. His goal while in college was to achieve sufficient financial success to have the option of retiring by the time he was thirty-five so that he could pursue other interests. Following a three-point plan, which is described in chapter 2, "Choosing Your Destination," he realized his goal.

By the time Lyle reached his goal, he realized that he thrived on the thrill and challenge of entrepreneurism, so he has continued to cofound, invest in, consult with and/or serve as a director for many new business ventures. However, Lyle now enjoys a fulfilling balance between personal and business interests. He now has time to actively participate in raising his two young children with his wife, Linda, as well as time to travel, write this book, give lectures for the benefit of other entrepreneurs, and enjoy a wide variety of recreational activities.

Dianne Mayfield believes that it is never too late to follow your heart and pursue your dreams. She began her entrepreneurial adventures at the age of thirty-five. While in her late twenties, Dianne chose to pursue a career as an attorney. Upon receiving her law degree from Washington University, she practiced law with a large firm and served as in-house counsel to a real estate franchise corporation. Then, in her mid-thirties, she decided to trade the security of a steady salary for the challenge, freedom and fulfillment of establishing her own law firm in the Washington, D.C. area.

Through her firm, Dianne has provided legal and business advice to a broad diversity of businesses, ranging from start-up operations to "Fortune 500" companies. In addition to practicing law, she has participated as a cofounder and key executive in a number of other entrepreneurial endeavors, including a franchise consulting firm, publishing company and dining/health club for business executives.

As a frequent speaker before business and college groups, Dianne encourages her listeners to have the courage to express their business creativity and the foresight to control their risks while doing so.

Now Los-Angeles based Lyle and Washington D.C.-based Dianne have teamed up to found Venture Services Group$^{SM}$, a consulting company catering to the growing business. Venture Services Group has assembled a team of skilled professionals who help businesses successfully make transitions through the various stages of growth.

## *Road Map Format*

You may skim a road map for a general perspective concerning a particular trip or point of interest, or you may carefully study a map to discover details and various travel options for a proposed journey. This road map is designed to serve both purposes.

Each chapter begins with a "Chapter Destination" that capsulizes where the chapter is headed.

Bold headnotes highlight points of interest within chapter sub-sections. The "Summary Tour" at the end of each chapter revisits key points. This format was chosen so that the book might not only be read word-for-word, but also might serve as a desk reference for basic principles to guide decisions.

## *Enjoy the Journey!*

❖ **The goal should not only be to end up with a successful business but also to enjoy the journey.**

As we begin our trek, we wish to emphasize one important traveling ground rule. Namely, the goal should not only be to end up with a successful business but also to enjoy the journey.

The journey from the idea stage to a successfully operating business may be a long one. Some businesses take years to succeed, while others never achieve the hoped-for level of success. Neither this book nor any other source can guarantee business success. There is always the risk that an entrepreneur will not reach his or her desired destination.

Attaining success, however, should not be the only goal in starting a business. The journey, itself, holds many adventures and opportunities for fulfillment. Savor the pleasure of each successful stride and the invaluable benefits of the lessons learned from any faltering steps along the way.

*Summary Tour*

- Being an entrepreneur is the natural thing to do.

- If you have the drive to create, find an outlet for it, whether within your own business or within the business of another.

- **ENJOY THE JOURNEY!**

*As you begin your journey, don't worry about getting lost. There may be unexpected detours or wrong turns, from time to time, but those should not stop you from reaching your destination. That's why we call this book a road map – to help you get back on course.*

# Chapter 1

# The Entrepreneurial Traveler
## (A Profile of the Entrepreneur)

## Chapter Destination

*What is required to be a successful entrepreneur? This chapter examines ten personal traits that are useful, and often essential, for the entrepreneurial traveler to take along on the journey to ensure success.*

## The Meaning of "Entrepreneur"

*Webster's New World Dictionary* (1982 edition) defines *entrepreneur* as "a person who organizes and manages a business undertaking, assuming the risk for the sake of profit." The word derives from the french word *entreprendre*, which means "to undertake."

A definition, such as the one above, merely describes the external results of what the entrepreneur does. This chapter goes a step further by exploring selected attributes and qualities of the entrepreneurial traveler that lead to successful experiences and enjoyable journeys.

There is no stereotypical entrepreneur. Being an entrepreneur is not related to age or background. As discussed in the preceding chapter, being an entrepreneur is a very natural thing to do. People discover their entrepreneurial instinct at many different ages. Some discover it while still a child and simply continue the process as an adult. Others do not discover it until they have already pursued a career as an employee – then, at some point they realize that they would prefer developing and running their own business rather than working for someone else. Others enjoy and want to keep their primary career but would like to express their creativity and enhance their earning potential either by functioning as an "intrapreneur" within their employer's business or by starting a business that they can operate in their free time. For example, a school teacher with blocks of free time – breaks and vacations – may want to test the entrepreneurial waters during those work breaks.

Although there is no stereotypical entrepreneur, there are certain attributes, ten of which are described below, that are commonly found in successful entrepreneurs. If you don't feel strong in all these areas, that doesn't mean that you should avoid pursuing an entrepreneur's journey. In fact, very few entrepreneurs, if any, excel in all of these areas. The attributes may be learned, or they may be found in business partners selected to share the journey with you.

## *Belief in the Idea and in Yourself*

❖   **Dare to dream.**

❖   **Satisfy yourself that your idea has true market potential.**

❖   **Believe in and think for yourself.**

❖   **Pursue ideas that are of interest and value to you.**

❖   **Exude confidence.**

Every business begins with an idea. **Every product and service** that you use daily and **every office, store and factory** started as an entrepreneur's dream. For example, Ford Motor Company did not just appear on this planet with billions of dollars a year in sales. Somewhere back in time, Henry Ford sat around trying to figure out how to build a better car. IBM was a start-up business at one point and, more recently, Apple Computer and Compaq Computer were entrepreneurs' ideas that quickly turned into multi-billion dollar businesses. If all of these started simply as ideas, why shouldn't you be able to develop your dreams and ideas into successful products and businesses, too?

Of course, not every idea has the potential for success. For your idea to become a successful business, you must believe in that idea to your very core. A tenacious belief in the idea is essential for mentally weathering the storms and roadblocks that often beset the entrepreneurial traveler.

A key to believing in a business idea is to be convinced that the idea has true market potential. You must research and assess the market potential for your business idea with optimism but also with realism. Chapter 2, "Choosing Your Destination," provides guidance for assessing the viability of business ideas.

Once you are convinced that your idea has sound market potential, you must remain committed to the pursuit of that idea in order for it to become a successful venture. Commitment to the pursuit of that idea requires a belief in yourself as the person who can successfully implement it. Belief in your ability to successfully implement the business idea comes from understanding yourself, choosing ideas that are of interest and value to you and independent thinking.

Becoming an entrepreneur requires careful self-evaluation. The better you understand yourself, the more likely you are to select a business idea that is natural and enjoyable for you. Also, the better you understand yourself and know your strengths and weaknesses, the easier it will be to know when to rely on others in the process of building your business.

Of course, there are other less controllable factors, such as luck and timing, that affect the success of a business venture and the speed with which it is implemented. Self-evaluation, however, is a crucial element for ensuring that you will be happy with your choice and that the venture will develop as smoothly as possible.

One key to developing belief in oneself is to be an independent thinker. You must step back from all the other input from parents, family and friends and make a decision based on what you believe you would truly enjoy the most. Rather than follow our own inner desires, all too frequently we choose our professional roads based upon our observations of others as we are growing up, our perception of what others expect of us, or our desire to project a particular image or achieve a particular lifestyle. Hopefully, the decisions we make lead to professions that we truly enjoy. All too often, however, we may reach our professional goal only to realize that we do not enjoy what we are doing because our choice is not in line with our own internal preferences.

The successful entrepreneur, at some point in his or her development, faces these career decisions head-on and has the courage (and/or the luck and opportunity) to implement them. It is never too late to make these decisions, but the earlier they are made, the more time the decision-maker will have to enjoy their benefits. One of the goals of this road map is to facilitate the decision-making process.

Consider the number of hours that you spend every day in your profession. At least half, and often more, of your waking hours are spent at work. If you do not enjoy what you are doing, consider the percentage of your life that you are spending in an unfulfilling manner. Why not choose to spend that time doing something that you will enjoy – something that is meaningful and fulfilling to you?

Some people pursue a particular idea solely because they believe it is an excellent way to make money, even though they really have no interest in or knowledge of the business selected. This is one of the most common causes of failure. To be successful, you should have both an interest and at least some knowledge about the area in which you wish to become involved. You can't just look at someone else making money and plan on imitating what that person has done without exploring what's involved.

Just because your friend, Bob, opened a little restaurant and became a financial success does not mean that you should do the same thing. Maybe Bob loved to cook and socialize, had family connections and acquired a lease in the best part of town. You must be aware of all the elements that come into play to make a success. You must understand your own interests, strong points and weaknesses. Well-intentioned people may fail just by virtue of being a "copycat" rather than a true entrepreneur. There is nothing wrong with going into a business similar to someone else's. In fact, many successful businesses have been built by taking an existing idea for a business and then improving the product or providing a better service. Just be sure that the business you choose is the right one for you.

If you have never tried being an entrepreneur and you want measurable guidance as to your strengths, weaknesses and potential for success, there are a number of tests that allow you to measure your "entrepreneurial quotient." However, a few words of caution are in order concerning these tests – they should be used only as a starting point for your evaluation process, not as a roadblock to your intentions. If you have a good idea for a product or business, have done your homework to determine the market and profit potential and have developed a plan for financing and development, there is no reason why you should not "go for it." If you lack some of the qualities that the entrepreneur tests indicate you should have, you can always acquire those qualities or find a business partner who possesses them.

If you truly believe in your idea and in yourself as the person to implement it, you will automatically feel a certain confidence about pursuing your goals. Exude that confidence, for it is that confidence that will lead others to also believe in and support your venture.

## Simplicity/Big-Picture Orientation

❖    **Always keep sight of the big picture.**

❖    **Keep it simple.**

Starting and operating any business involves many detailed steps. Sometimes when an entrepreneur starts dealing with the detail, he or she loses sight of the end goal of the business. This can be fatal to the business. The entrepreneur must always keep the "big picture" of the business in sight for guidance in making wise decisions about the smaller details. The best way to do this is to keep everything as simple as possible. The simpler the structure, the less likely the detail will become overwhelming and the less likely the entrepreneur will lose sight of the big picture.

As an entrepreneur, you will be constantly confronted with more tasks than you and your limited staff can possibly perform. Therefore, you must keep your principal business goals firmly in focus and not get sidetracked with nonessential work.

Unfortunately, there will almost always be some diversions demanding your attention that will necessarily shift your focus from the primary business goals. For example, a cash crisis to meet payroll and pay vendors or employee relations issues can require almost full attention until resolved. The successful entrepreneur will anticipate these sorts of problems and will manage the business so as to minimize their occurrence and facilitate their resolution. We will discuss how to do this throughout the book.

Any time you feel too consumed by the details of your business, the best course of action may be to temporarily step back and view the business from the perspective of an independent, outside observer. By doing so, you may spot important adjustments that will keep the business on course for success.

## *Creativity*

❖   **Exercise creativity at all stages of the journey.**

❖   **Look for a market niche and develop a creative way to fill that niche.**

❖   **Think beyond the barriers of tradition.**

Being an entrepreneur calls for creativity at all stages of the journey.

For example, in choosing a business idea, the successful entrepreneur identifies an unfulfilled market need or desire shared by many – a market niche – and then creatively devises a way to fill that niche by satisfying the need or desire at a price people are willing to pay.

Once a business has been launched, there are countless opportunities for the entrepreneur to exercise creativity in building the business. There is no "one way" in which a business should be built or a problem resolved, so the entrepreneur is constantly faced with opportunities to be creative. Sometimes the best solution for a problem is an approach that is totally unconventional and non-traditional. The creative entrepreneur is able to think of out-of-the-ordinary solutions when necessary.

Creativity often defies definition. When it happens, we know it, but we may be hard-pressed to describe exactly how it happened. Creative thinking often seems to magically emerge, sometimes when we least expect it. For example, the discovery of the product "Scotchgard" reportedly resulted from an accidental, creative observation. A laboratory assistant for the 3M Corporation observed that a fluid she spilled on her sneakers kept clean the spot where she had spilled it. The fluid was being developed for aircraft use, but the lab assistant's observation led to the discovery of a new use and market for the product. Now Scotchgard is widely used to protect clothing, carpeting, upholstery and a wide array of consumer and commercial goods.

Creativity cannot be forced, but it can be facilitated by adopting certain attitudes and practices. To be creative, we must allow ourselves to think beyond the barriers of tradition. Much of our life is spent learning how things "should" be done. We learn rules and routines that create mental barriers which can stifle creativity. Being creative requires breaking through these mental barriers and viewing a challenge or issue from a different perspective, with "new eyes."

A naval engineer observed torsion springs, used on board ship, fall and bounce. When, as a result of his observation, he came up with the idea for the toy, Slinky, he was not thinking in traditional terms. He allowed himself to think creatively.

The creative person is not afraid to think of and express ideas that may seem unusual, bizarre or outrageous to other people. If Slinky's inventor had been afraid of promoting his idea, millions of his

product would never have been sold worldwide.
Also, the creative person is not afraid to have lots of
ideas fail or be discarded. Sometimes it is necessary to
try many ideas before finding one that works well.

Sometimes, the best way to foster creativity is to
not try too hard. This may mean leaving a problem
for a while, relaxing, taking a vacation or otherwise
turning attention to something else. Some people
have even found sleeping to work wonders for creativity. It is said that Thomas Edison frequently
dozed for hours while working on his inventions.
The creative part of our minds often works best
when we give it free rein to perform intuitively and
naturally.

## Flexible Planning

❖ Plan your journey and replan after every major
change.

❖ Write down your goals and visions.

❖ Expect the unexpected.

❖ Always have contingency plans.

Successful entrepreneurs are usually good planners. A new business is filled with potential opportunities for dispersion of energy, time and money.
For this reason, setting and following a **flexible** plan
is critical for success. (See the chapter on business
planning, "Planning Your Itinerary.")

Entrepreneurs are often considered visionaries.
For those visions to become realities, it is vital for the
entrepreneur to write down his or her visions and

goals for the business. This not only keeps the entrepreneur focused but also constantly reminds everyone else where the business is headed.

When starting a business, it is important to understand that the business is a growing, changing entity. No matter how carefully a business plan is formulated, circumstances will occur that will divert the plan from its original path. Therefore, you will find it necessary not only to plan your journey but also to replan after every major change. The most successful entrepreneurs are the ones who have the flexibility to quickly respond in positive and creative ways to changes that affect the business. They acknowledge in advance that change is inevitable. Then they organize the business and condition themselves and key employees to accept and manage the changes.

As you proceed, expect the unexpected. Understand that when you structure a business plan or strategy, there are many variables that you may not foresee or over which you have no control. No doubt, some of these variables will cause changes in your direction as you implement your plan or strategy. Having this understanding will help you avoid becoming immobilized by the occurrence of the unexpected.

Always have contingency plans. There is never just one way to accomplish one's goals. In implementing any particular phase of a business, one way to avoid frustration over the failure of one strategy is to have multiple strategies. That way, if one fails, there are others to take its place. For example, if you do not secure financing from the source that you expected, have several other sources that you have already targeted to approach. Similarly, arrange for more than one vendor to supply vital inventory items.

Both planning and flexibility are critical to avoid becoming lost. Detours are usually affordable, but getting lost may mean the end of the journey.

## Optimism

❖ **Look for positive opportunities in every seemingly negative occurrence.**

❖ **If one approach fails, try another.**

Optimism is an essential quality for overcoming roadblocks on the entrepreneur's journey. It is a quality that can turn a potential hassle or disaster into a positive experience. Optimism is invaluable for dealing with the inevitable rejections and obstacles that are intrinsic to starting and operating businesses. Also, optimism inspires employees and business associates to feel good about the business and their role in it.

Optimism is just a matter of perspective – a way of looking at things. The optimist looks for positive opportunities in every seemingly negative occurrence. The optimist realizes that there are countless alternatives for reaching a goal or solving a problem and that, if one fails, there are many others that will succeed in its place. The optimist does not view so-called "failure" as a devastating occurrence but, rather, learns from the experience and tries again with a different approach.

Of course, there is a difference between the optimism that will promote success and "blind optimism," which can lead to failure. Optimism must be tempered with realism. The optimism that we are referring to is a positive and self-confident outlook on life and the business – an attitude that the glass is half full instead of half empty.

## Realism

❖  **Maintain a realistic perspective.**

❖  **Set realistic goals and timetables.**

The entrepreneur must be the ultimate dreamer, but tempered with reasoned realism. If the entrepreneur is not a dreamer and creator, the business idea will never be conceived and developed. If the entrepreneur is not also realistic, however, the road to realizing the dream will be treacherous. For example, entrepreneurs who are not realistic in estimating the market potential for their business ideas may spend years developing a product or business only to learn that there is not enough demand to ever generate a profit.

Maintaining a realistic perspective helps avoid the disappointment and frustration that result from unattainable expectations. A key to maintaining a realistic perspective is to realize that success does not mean winning 100% of the time. Rather, success means winning more than you lose and picking the right things to go for. There are many roads and detours on the journey to success. Always keep looking ahead. It is dangerous to dwell on today's successes and failures. The world is dynamic and things can change very quickly from good to bad or bad to good.

Realism is particularly important in setting goals and time deadlines. Often, being an entrepreneur involves a sense of urgency. There are sales goals and projections to meet, projects to complete, and countless other deadline-oriented aspects to starting and successfully operating a business. The realism with which the entrepreneur views and communicates the deadlines for these tasks can mean the difference between a pleasurable, fulfilling business endeavor and a frustrating, stressful experience. Everything has a gestation period. Acknowledge this fact and try to build realistic expectations for project timetables in order to avoid frustration and discouragement.

## Communication

❖    **Communicate your ideas clearly, with commitment and enthusiasm.**

❖    **Understand the ultimate goal of the communication and then prepare, prepare, prepare yourself to meet that goal.**

Entrepreneurs need to be good communicators. They must repeatedly communicate and sell their ideas to sources of financing, potential customers, vendors, business partners and employees.

In the beginning, a business is nothing more than an idea. It is the communication of the idea that begins to give form and substance to the business. One of the keys to effective communication of the idea is believing in the idea and in yourself, as discussed above. The more you, personally, believe in the value of the idea and believe that you are the person to implement it, the more easily you will be able to sell the idea to others. You're always the salesperson of your idea, even if you think you are just the inventor of your idea.

Communication is important not only in the beginning stages of the business, but also in later stages. As discussed further in the chapter on management techniques ("Staying on Course"), one element of effective management is to clearly communicate to employees and associates the goals of the company and the role expectations for each employee. It is also important to communicate constructive feedback concerning job performance.

To effectively communicate, you must clearly understand the goal or purpose of your communication and then structure your presentation to optimally meet that goal or purpose. Sometimes a simple, well-thought-out, verbal communication will suffice. Some circumstances, however, such as a presentation to raise money or market your product, may require a visual display to support your verbal communication. Prototypes, sketches, graphs, photographs, or other visual effects may create a vivid and memorable image of your business and your concept of its planned growth. One of the secrets for successful communication is to understand the ultimate goal of the communication and then to prepare, prepare, prepare your presentation to meet that goal.

Preparation includes not only preparing a description of your business or product, but also developing an understanding of the needs and perspectives of the party to whom you are communicating.

If the goal is to sell your product to a particular type of customer, you should first research and understand the needs of this customer base. Then, your presentation should be designed to demonstrate all the ways that your product meets those needs.

If the goal of your presentation is to raise money, try to cover all possible questions that might be raised by prospective investors. State the purpose, amount, structure and timing of the investment. Convey all of the reasons why this business opportunity is positioned to succeed, as well as possible risks. Provide enough information to elicit a simple "yes" or "no" response from prospective investors rather than a discussion (to find out information that you should have conveyed in your presentation).

One of the best ways to be a successful communicator is to place yourself in the position of the intended listener. What are your listener's needs and preferences? What type of information does that listener need in hear or see in order to respond as you prefer?

## Risk-Taking

❖ **Accept the fact that starting a business involves an element of risk, but learn to manage the risks by understanding what they are and then limiting the "down side" of those risks.**

Every entrepreneurial venture involves some element of risk. Being an entrepreneur means learning to accept these risks as part of the process of achieving one's goals, while at the same time learning to manage and limit their down side.

What level of risk do you feel comfortable with? Everyone has his or her own unique risk tolerance level, which can even vary within the same individual, depending upon what that person stands to gain or lose at any point in time. A person may feel much more comfortable venturing forward to start a business when he or she is single, with few family or financial obligations, rather than when he or she has a family to support, mortgage payments to meet, and various other financial obligations requiring a dependable monthly income.

If you want to express your entrepreneurial drive, but you are not comfortable with the anticipated risks, look for ways to limit those risks. Perhaps you could cut back on certain expenses, divest yourself of unnecessary financial obligations or find ways to supplement your income while starting the business. Or, instead of becoming an entrepreneur at this time, consider becoming an intrapreneur. Develop your product or idea with the support of your employer or another company that would profit from its implementation.

If you fear the risks, just realize that the worst that can happen is that the venture won't succeed. If your endeavor fails, you may end up with a bruised ego and, perhaps, some money lost. The experience, however, can still be more of a gain than a loss if you limit your risks in ways described in this book. Learning and growth come from failures, as well as from successes. Today's failed venture may be the learning experience that will make possible tomorrow's incredibly successful enterprise. Remember the adage, "It is better to have tried and failed than never to have tried at all."

The stories behind some of the most successful entrepreneurs reveal that, before achieving "success," those entrepreneurs had more than their share of "failures." What ultimately made them successful was learning from their failures, picking themselves up and trying again. One of the greatest inventors of all time, Thomas Edison, spent ten years making continuous mistakes before discovering how to make a nickel alkaline storage battery. When questioned about making so many mistakes and having so many failures, Edison reportedly responded, "Fail! What

are you talking about? Today I know 25,000 ways not
to make a battery!" Edison never once thought of any
of his unsuccessful attempts as failures, but as learning.

Whether your endeavor succeeds or fails, you
will experience valuable gains – especially the
knowledge that you can have mobility, freedom, creative fulfillment and control over your own destiny.
You will no longer feel tied to a particular position. If
your venture does not succeed, you may choose to return to a less risky, more conservative path, but you
will never feel forced to remain an unwilling captive
of a position in which you are not happy. You will
have tested the path of the entrepreneur, learned
some lessons from your initial journey and will
know that you can always pursue an entrepreneurial
venture again.

## *Persistence*

❖    **Keep your attention focused on the business.**

❖    **Never, never, never give up (as long as you believe there is valid market potential for your
business product or service).**

❖    **Keep exploring solutions until the solution fits
the problem.**

Every step of the entrepreneur's journey calls
for persistence and perseverance. It took twenty-two
years before the creator of Xerox technology saw his
idea in the marketplace. The man who invented
laser technology waited twenty years before a patent
was issued for his creation.

Fortunately, not every venture requires quite as much time, but every venture calls for persistence at some stage. At the idea stage, persistence is required to avoid talking yourself out of a good idea. Once the business is launched, persistence is essential to continue the building process and to find resolutions for the numerous challenges that arise.

One element of persistence is the ability to focus attention on a single project (your business) for a sustained period of time. A business cannot succeed overnight. Three to five years of focused attention are usually required to grow a business from an idea into a sustainably profitable entity. If you divert your focus from the development of the business, the business simply will not develop.

Another element of persistence is to never, never, never give up. To sustain this sort of persistence, the entrepreneur must possess an undaunted belief in and commitment to the business concept and a strong sense of perseverance. Of course, in some instances it may be inappropriate to remain persistent. If the business concept does not realistically have the market potential that the entrepreneur thought it would or if the market changes, the wisest business judgment may be to discontinue the business endeavor or to drastically change directions. As long as the entrepreneur sees realistic market potential for the business, however, persistence and commitment will be required to ensure its success.

Persistence does not mean butting your head against a wall trying to force a specific solution to a problem to work. Perhaps the solution you thought was the right one just won't work. Persistence means trying many different solutions until you find the ones that work – keep exploring solutions until the solution fits the problem.

Persistence must be applied to each functional area of the business – financing, marketing, and every other operational area – even if the entrepreneur wears all the hats. Persistence must be blended with intelligent goals, creativity and good planning to achieve workable solutions and success.

## Action-Orientation

❖ **Be a doer.**

❖ **Be a decision-maker.**

Being an entrepreneur calls for self-evaluation and planning, but it also requires action. Before starting a business, evaluate yourself, your situation in life and your goals. Make a decision and a plan to start a particular type of business based on that evaluation. Then just do it – start the business. You can't analyze and plan forever. The business will never become a reality until you take action to start it.

Entrepreneurs are dreamers, but they are also doers. At some point the focus must shift from creating ideas to taking action. At some point you must get started. Once you have started, you will shift back and forth between ideas and action, but the action will never stop, unless you close the business or attain such success that you are able to sell it.

Successful entrepreneurs have the courage and conviction to make decisions and to make them relatively quickly. They realize that any decision is better than no decision. Some people just cannot seem to make a decision without exhaustive research, study and collaboration with others. Realizing the importance of making a decision and moving ahead, the entrepreneur has the ability to make a decision quickly based upon the best available information at the time. He or she also possesses the insight and foresight to leave the door open so that decisions can be quickly changed or modified as new knowledge is gained.

Being action-oriented is what distinguishes the successful entrepreneur from the wishful thinker.

## Summary Tour

Being an entrepreneur is primarily a frame of mind, an attitude. If you have decided to make the entrepreneur's journey, taking along the following ten qualities will enhance your potential for success:

### BELIEF IN THE IDEA AND IN YOURSELF

- Dare to dream.
- Satisfy yourself that your idea has true market potential.
- Believe in and think for yourself.
- Pursue ideas that are of interest and value to you.
- Exude confidence.

### SIMPLICITY/BIG-PICTURE ORIENTATION

- Always keep sight of the big picture.
- Keep it simple.

## CREATIVITY

- Exercise creativity at all stages of the journey.
- Look for a market niche and develop a creative way to fill that niche.
- Think beyond the barriers of tradition.

## FLEXIBLE PLANNING

- Plan your journey and replan after every major change.
- Write down your goals and visions.
- Expect the unexpected.
- Always have contingency plans.

## OPTIMISM

- Look for positive opportunities in every seemingly negative occurrence.
- If one approach fails, try another.

## REALISM

- Maintain a realistic perspective.
- Set realistic goals and timetables.

## COMMUNICATION

- Communicate your ideas clearly, with commitment and enthusiasm.
- Understand the ultimate goal of the communication and then prepare, prepare, prepare yourself to meet that goal.

## RISK-TAKING

- Accept the fact that starting a business involves an element of risk, but learn to manage the risks by understanding what they are and then limiting the "down side" of those risks.

## PERSISTENCE

- Keep your attention focused on the business.
- Never, never, never give up (as long as you believe there is valid market potential for your business product or service).
- Keep exploring solutions until the solution fits the problem.

## ACTION ORIENTATION

- Be a doer.
- Be a decision-maker.

# Chapter 2

# Choosing Your Destination
## (Selecting a Business Idea)

## Chapter Destination

*The first leg of your entrepreneurial journey involves choosing your destination — the business you will build. This chapter provides guidance for making that decision. If you have already selected your business idea or are already involved in an entrepreneurial venture, then you may want to skip this chapter and go on to others that relate to other topics that are of interest to you.*

## The Basics

❖ Choose a business that is a good match with your personality and interests.

❖ Choose a business that has market and profit potential equal to or greater than your financial expectations.

❖   **Choose a business with a very specific market niche.**

The business you choose to pursue should satisfy several basic criteria. Although these criteria may seem simplistic and obvious, they are often ignored or overlooked.

First, the business should be a good match with your personality and interests. It should involve an area you enjoy and, preferably, an area in which you have knowledge and experience. Starting and building a successful business requires a tremendous commitment of your time and energy. If you don't have a genuine interest in the venture you have chosen – perhaps because you chose it only to make money – you'll find it extraordinarily difficult to sustain the commitment required to make the business a success.

In addition to having a genuine interest in the business concept, the more you know about the business and the more experience you have in the industry selected, the easier your journey to success will be. If, for example, you want to become a home builder, your chances of success will be much greater if you have been employed in the building industry; have learned how to manage subcontractors; and know where to purchase building materials at the best price. If you have no experience in the building industry, you will be faced with two learning curves instead of just one: learning how to build homes and learning how to start and run a business.

If you are absolutely certain that you want to start a business in a field in which you have extraordinary interest but no experience, there are ways to do so while minimizing the risks associated with your lack of experience. For instance, you could become employed in the field for a long enough period to learn the "tricks of the trade" or you could find a business partner or hire a manager who has the needed experience. Still another option may be to retain your current source of income, while taking steps to learn the needed skills on a part-time basis. Using our home-building example, you might work part-time (evenings and weekends) with a builder, take courses related to home-building, or actually begin building your first house by managing the subcontractors in your spare time, while retaining your current salaried position.

A second essential criterion for selecting a business is to choose one that has market and profit potential equal to or greater than your financial expectations. It's a terrible shock to find out after years of work that success within your chosen field does not come close to meeting your financial goals and expectations. Having your business fail is certainly a disappointment but, perhaps, as great a disappointment is for your business to succeed, only to discover that such success does not generate sufficient monetary rewards to meet your expectations.

Sufficient financial reward may be different for each entrepreneur. Some may be satisfied with a modest but stable income combined with the freedom of being self-employed; others may want the wealth and power associated with running a multi-million dollar business; while still others may seek wealth only, letting others actually run their business. One goal is not better than another. The key is to have your business choice be consistent with your desires. It is better to realistically analyze the potential for a business idea before you pursue it than to devote months or years to the development of the idea before realizing that the business will never meet your financial expectations.

Many people fall in love with and pursue a business idea without realistically considering its profit potential. Developing a business that generates $100,000 per year in gross income and operates at a loss can consume as much time and energy as developing a business that generates $100,000,000 per year and operates at a profit. Before you pursue an idea, it's best to realistically assess the market demand for your product or service and estimate income and profits to determine if the idea has the potential for meeting your financial and other goals. The chapters on marketing ("Designing the Tour Package") and business planning ("Planning Your Itinerary") provide guidance for analyzing the market, income and profit potential for the business.

A third criterion for selecting a business is to choose a business that fills a very specific market niche. The more narrowly defined the market niche, the easier the marketing of the product will be and the more likely the product will succeed. This concept is discussed in greater detail in the chapter on marketing ("Designing the Tour Package").

All of the above criteria are essential for raising capital to finance the business. Investors generally want more than just a good idea – they want expertise, commitment, and solid profit and market potential. Without these elements, a great idea, in and of itself, will sometimes be enough to get the business financed. However, you may be required to give up more control and ownership than you would if all of the suggested elements were present.

## *Discovering Business Ideas*

❖ **If you want to start a business but you don't have a specific idea in mind, the best approach is to develop a specific frame of mind. Tell your subconscious mind that you want a business idea and then use every possible opportunity to watch for ideas.**

Maybe you haven't the slightest idea what kind of business you want to develop. Perhaps you feel an overwhelming drive to create, but haven't pinpointed how to express it; or perhaps you are bored or disillusioned with what you are doing and you want to try something new. You are saying to yourself, "If only I could come up with a business idea and start my own business. I know I could be successful. I'm hard working, I'm diligent, I'm creative. I just need a product idea."

If you want to start a business but you don't have a specific idea in mind, the best approach is to develop a specific frame of mind. Tell your subconscious mind that you want a business idea and then use every possible opportunity to watch for ideas.

There are countless business opportunities everywhere, just waiting for the observant and creative mind to bring them to life. These ideas are there for you to discover while you are simply living your day-to-day life – driving to work; taking your kids to soccer practice; washing the dishes; going to a restaurant, the beach, or the movies; or watching T.V. The idea for the microwave oven occurred to its inventor, Dr. Percy Spencer, in the 1940's when he walked in front of a radar antenna and the candy bar in his pocket melted. This seemingly insignificant occurrence gave him the idea of using microwaves to heat food. By the late 1980's approximately six out of every ten homes had a microwave oven.

Maybe the idea that you are looking for will surface while you are engaged in one of your favorite leisure-time activities. While singing in his church choir, a creative intrapreneur, Art Frye, saw the need for a bookmark that wouldn't fall out of his hymnal. Mr. Frye, who was a researcher for 3M, then developed the idea for Post-it brand notes and the rest is history. It's hard to imagine now how we ever got along without the colorful self-sticking notes.

Look at your own leisure activities and try to spot market needs. If you like to read in your spare time, ask yourself, "What would make reading better?" or "What would I enjoy doing associated with reading that other people will pay for?" Maybe you want to create a reading lamp that clips onto your book, or a chain of bookstores that have the ambiance of a warm and cozy private library, or a mail-order company that sells books, or a publishing company.

Perhaps while you are working, the idea will occur to you of a better, quicker way to do something. A secretary, Bette Nesmith, who knew the pain and anguish of correcting mistakes on typed pages, came up with the idea of a liquid correction fluid (now known as "Liquid Paper") that eventually developed into a multi-million dollar business. She and the other product developers mentioned above did not go out looking for a "glitzy" idea for a business. They found products that satisfied basic needs. Products that satisfy such basic needs often have incredibly broad market appeal.

Many people have found success by taking existing products and either improving them or marketing them differently. Look at what has happened in the consumer electronics field. Popular items like T.V.'s and stereos are constantly being modified or improved to generate new sales. We now have T.V.'s that are small enough to fit in your pocket or large enough to fill up practically an entire wall.

Cookies and ice cream are products which have been around for a long time. Yet the creators of such products as Mrs. Fields Cookies and Baskin-Robbins Ice Cream distinguished their products by marketing them differently. Rather than sell their cookies and ice cream through grocery stores, they set up their own storefronts featuring just their products. These companies may not have been the first to use this approach. However, their timing, entrepreneurial vision and drive led to success on a large scale. These entrepreneurs became leaders in changing their industries.

At first, it takes practice to develop the mindset to look for business ideas. But, with focus and practice, the process can become second nature to you. Maybe your friends and family would also enjoy becoming involved in the process. Perhaps while you are standing in line at the theater or sitting in a restaurant, you could swap business ideas. "If this restaurant owner were clever, he would attract more business by putting up a canopy, or changing the menu this way, or using this promotional campaign.... Did you see the article in the newspaper about the problem the people in the Northwest are having? What they need to solve that problem is _____....," etc.

Successful business ideas are those which: (1) solve a widely-shared problem or need (air conditioners); (2) provide a better way to accomplish a particular task (disposable razors and ball-point pens); or (3) for some other reason cause people to want to

spend their money on your product or service. Perhaps the product or service saves time (fast food
restaurants), entertains in a new and different way
(VCR's), has snob appeal (certain brands of clothing),
or takes care of routine responsibilities that are a
chore for the consumer (dishwashers and home
cleaning services).

The number of business opportunities is limitless. Opportunies lie both in the creation of entirely
new industries (as was originally the case with micro-
computers and fast food chains) and in finding new
niches in existing industries (as was the case with
pizza delivery services and quality-built small automobiles). Within a particular industry there are
countless sub-categories that entrepreneurs have discovered and are continuing to discover. For example,
within the microcomputer field are software developers, hardware manufacturers, printer and other peripheral manufacturers, trade magazines, trade
shows, authors and distributors, to name a few.

Entrepreneurs creating businesses within new
and emerging industries often find that, because of
the immature development of their industry, numerous opportunities arise in addition to their original ideas. These entrepreneurs may have found the
success of their original business threatened by the
lack of adequate support services (advertising firms,
publications, financing) and sales distribution channels (distributors, retail outlets, etc.). They, therefore,
may have been tempted or compelled to create additional ventures to facilitate their primary goal – the
success of their original business.

The founders of Ashton-Tate, the manufacturer
of the extremely successful dBASE database manager,
at one time owned a number of other companies, including a chain of retail software sales stores, a distri-

bution company and a mail-order company. When Ashton-Tate was first founded, the microcomputer industry was in its infancy, so the company created this infrastructure of other companies to help sell its products. The founders were classic entrepreneurs. They were persistent, creative and did not let the shortcomings of their emerging industry prevent their success.

Although many successful business ideas have been discovered by chance, it is also possible to adopt a planned approach to choosing a business. One of the coauthors of this book, Lyle Maul, did just that. While in college, he set a personal goal of achieving sufficient financial success to have the option of retiring by the age of thirty-five. Achievement of this goal was accomplished via the following three-point plan: (1) Select two "hot" industries in which to become knowledgeable. (He chose health care and micro-computers.) (2) Learn the business firsthand in small to medium-sized companies within the selected industries, concentrating on financing and marketing. (3) Create entrepreneurial businesses on the side to accumulate capital for future opportunities and to experiment firsthand on a small scale. While following this three-point plan, Lyle was able to spot the market niches that could be filled by businesses that became successful enough to meet his personal and financial goals.

A key to selecting a new idea within an existing industry is to analyze the industry and find a niche that needs a new or improved product or service. Become familiar with the target industry by taking a full- or part-time job with a company in that industry or by being active in clubs or associations within the industry. Then watch for the opportunities.

Are you interested in discovering an undeveloped or underdeveloped niche within a new growth industry? One approach is to select a mature, prosperous industry and completely analyze and dissect the many categories of businesses within it. Then compare that analysis to the new growth industry. For example, if you are interested in finding a business niche in the microcomputer field, analyze another established industry that might have similar target markets, such as the mainframe computer industry, or even a completely unrelated industry, such as the record industry. Then compare your analysis of the established industry to the growth industry that you are evaluating for ideas of market niches that may not have been tapped or fully developed. This methodology is very effective for individuals who are already in growth industries and who want to participate more directly in the wealth being amassed by the entrepreneurs in it.

Also, remember that it is not always necessary to create a new market niche. It is also possible to become a new competitor in an existing market niche. Just because someone else was first does not mean it's too late for you to start a similar business. The second, third and other subsequent entrants into a market can learn a lot from the market-entry pioneer. These later entrants can improve upon the concept or appeal to a slightly different category within the niche by emphasizing different product features or using a different marketing tactic. If the pioneer does well, it is often easier for others to raise money and gain market acceptance.

## Analyzing the Options

❖ Assess your own time availability, financial resources, expertise, risk comfort-level and financial expectations. Then choose a business that is
the best match with your resources and expectations.

❖ Just as venture capital companies analyze hundreds of deals before committing money to a
particular one, you are, in a sense, a venture capitalist with your own time, money and energy to
invest. You should analyze your options carefully before committing yourself to one.

While you are looking for business ideas, you
will also need to be analyzing whether or not each
particular idea is a good one for you to pursue. Making the decision concerning which business to start
requires as much self-analysis as it does analysis of a
business idea. The goal should be to find a business
that is a good match with your interests, resources
and expectations. How much time do you have
available to devote to the business opportunity?
What kinds of financial resources are at your dis-
posal? If you need additional money, how are your
money-raising abilities? What is your level of expertise in the businesses you are considering? What
level of risk are you willing to assume? What kind of
financial returns do you expect?

It is not unusual to come up with an idea that
appears to be a winner, only to discover – after analyzing your interests and resources and considering
the market potential for the product – that the idea is
not appropriate for you to pursue. Don't be discour-

aged if you go through the analysis process scores of times before you find an idea that you want to develop. Just as venture capital companies analyze hundreds of deals before committing money to a particular one, you are, in a sense, a venture capitalist with your own time, money and energy to invest. You should analyze your options carefully before committing yourself to one.

Of course, we do not mean to encourage overanalysis to the point of never starting your journey. We only wish to encourage you to examine business opportunities from a variety of angles so that you will have realistic expectations and will be happy with the choice that you make.

The remainder of this subsection provides some guidance for analyzing business options. In a book of this scope, it is impossible to present detailed comparisons of every different type of business. Nevertheless, we can point out some questions to keep in mind when conducting your own analysis of a business idea.

Our discussion assumes that you are an aspiring entrepreneur, charged up with the idea of starting a business but uncertain in which industry, much less the specific type of business. Should you start a manufacturing, retail, service, distribution, publishing, real estate, mail-order, import/export or some other type of business?

Our goal is not to list or analyze all the business categories that exist. Rather, our goal is to help the aspiring entrepreneur realize that deciding which business to create is more than a product decision. You must consider the time and financial requirements of any business you are thinking of starting. You must also consider how much you know or need to learn about the business and the level of risk with which you feel comfortable.

Before beginning our discussion, we wish to stress the need to avoid stereotypes and to keep an open and creative mind when you are analyzing your options. To illustrate our points, we sometimes compare broad business categories, such as manufacturing, retail and service businesses. Actually, the decision to start a particular kind of business is rarely made by first trying to choose a category of business. Typically, the entrepreneur tries to select or unexpectedly discovers a particular business idea, then tries to determine if that idea is one that he or she wishes to pursue.

Do not be limited by the conclusions we may draw in our illustrations. Not all of our conclusions will apply to all businesses that might be classified within the category we are discussing. Furthermore, the traditional definitions of the categories we are comparing are changing dramatically. The definition of a category may not be as clear-cut as it may seem.

For example, the term "manufacturer" typically connotes an image of a large factory billowing smoke or a huge assembly-line operation. In today's world of sophisticated communication and high-speed transportation, however, a manufacturer may not resemble that image at all. A company in the United States might be called a manufacturer, yet may actually make no part of the product it "manufactures." The company may, instead, subcontract with other companies throughout the world that can make and assemble the product's components at a much lower cost than would be the case in the United States. In such cases, the term "manufacturer" refers to the company that owns the trademark, patent, copyright or licensing rights to the product; controls the design of the product; and controls the marketing, sales, service and distribution of the product. This type of manufacturer more closely resembles a service business than a traditional manufacturing business.

Likewise, the term "retailer" is commonly envisioned as a store-front stocked with various manufacturers' goods, waiting for customers to walk through the door to make a purchase. However, many of today's most successful retailers have aggressive mail-order/catalog and telemarketing operations through which they attempt to reach the customer at home or at work. Many retailers also play the role of manufacturer by making some of their own goods under the process commonly referred to as "private labeling."

Never be limited by category definitions. We have compared certain business categories just to illustrate how you might apply the analysis of options to the business you are considering. Do not let the traditional boundaries or limits of a particular business category confine the development or marketing of your products or services. Remember to always think creatively and think beyond the barriers of tradition.

This may sound simple, but you will find that there are many people and organizations that will continually try to categorize you and your business for their own needs. For example, the Internal Revenue Service, when assigning your Federal Tax Employer's Identification Number, will want to assign a "Business Code" category to your business. Trade magazines when writing about your product or your company will want to categorize you into a specific section of their publication. Investors and lenders will try to label your business for such purposes as determining appropriate price/earnings or debt-to-equity ratios. The end result is that only the entrepreneur with strong conviction and vision can filter the information from outsiders and keep pursuing his or her goal without becoming a ping-pong ball bouncing around and changing direction based on everyone else's input as to what the business should be.

## *Time Considerations*

Time considerations to take into account in selecting a business include: (1) the amount of time that you plan to devote to the development of the business, (2) whether or not the time demands of a particular business will allow you to live the kind of life style that you wish, (3) the amount of lead time that you can afford before the business begins to show a profit and (4) the lead time required to beat the competition to the marketplace and/or meet a specific seasonal buying period.

The amount of time that you plan to devote to the development of the business will be a major factor in determining the type of business to pursue. If you want to develop the business in your spare time while you maintain a full-time or part-time salaried position, then you will need to choose a business that lends itself to that sort of sporadic time commitment. If, on the other hand, you intend to devote full time to the business development, your options are much broader.

Even if you intend to devote full time to the development of the business, there are certain time considerations related to life style that you should keep in mind when selecting a business idea. For example, suppose, through your travels, you have fallen in love with country inns and have decided that your goal in life is to develop and run a country inn. Understand, realistically, that an owner/manager of a country inn may work 15 hours or more per day, 7 days a week, unless the inn generates sufficient revenue to compensate other people to cover shifts for the operation and management of the inn. Someone must be available to provide services from the time inn travelers get up in the morning until they go to bed at night. It may be much more romantic to be the traveler at the inn than it is to be the inn owner. The important point is for you to understand the time requirements of the business you are considering before you make the commitment to start the business. Will the time demands of the business allow you to live the kind of life style that you wish?

Another time-related issue to consider is the amount of lead time you can afford, both financially and from a time-commitment standpoint, before you receive a sufficient return to maintain or achieve your financial and personal goals and needs. Every business requires some amount of lead time before generating enough income to meet expenses and show a profit. The amount of such required lead time can vary from months to years, depending upon the type of business. You should develop a clear idea of the average lead time required before you start the business so that you will secure enough funds to carry you through the start-up phase. By accurately estimating lead time, you will also avoid the discouragement that could result from missing projected timetables.

Starting a manufacturing business may require six months to a year or more. It takes time to develop a product and set up reliable production, marketing and service functions. Most retail, service and mail-order businesses require less time to start than a manufacturing business. Launching a professional service business, for example, may take two or three months from the time the idea is conceived until the business is operational.

Sometimes the amount of lead time available for launching a business is controlled by the threat of a competitor racing with you to be first to the marketplace with a new product or by seasonal buying patterns, or both. If you have designed a widget to be sold primarily at Christmas-time through retail stores, retail store representatives may place all their orders for Christmas widgets prior to July 1 each year. If your product is not ready until July 31, you may have missed your sales opportunity for that year and you may not be able to market your product until next year. By that time, a competitor may have seen your widget and copied it or made a better one. In such a case, you will have lost an entire year's revenue and you may be in a much weaker competitive position.

If you are in danger of missing a seasonal buying deadline or being upstaged by a competitor, you should consider ways of modifying your plans to meet the target deadline dates. Perhaps you had planned to introduce a whole line of products but could, instead, introduce only a part now and the rest later. If you have developed a product that you feel needs refinement, perhaps you could introduce the current version, then develop upgrades, later versions, enhancements or other variations at a later date.

We do not mean to imply that you should cut corners and come out with a product that is of inferior quality. To do so might create generate a negative reputation for your products or your business that would be difficult to overcome. We merely suggest that there might be ways to introduce a quality product or service, but with fewer "bells and whistles" than you ultimately wish to include. The creativity and best judgment of the entrepreneur and the entrepreneur's management team will be required to assess the risks, options and trade-offs. There is generally no one "right" answer for what to do, but there are often ways to meet deadlines without compromising quality.

The best way to determine time-related factors associated with a particular type of business is to talk to other people who are in a similar business. You may also find it useful to  contact associations or trade groups whose members are in the type of business you are considering.

## Financing

How much money is needed to start the business you are considering – to acquire assets, inventory and supplies; hire employees; meet other start-up costs; and cover your own living expenses until the business is generating enough income to support you? Do you have enough money or credit to provide the initial financing, or will you need financing from other sources. If you need outside financing, are the prospective returns sufficient to interest investors and lenders? For additional guidance on financing the business, see the chapter, "Financing the Expedition."

Manufacturing businesses often require substantial sums of money to start and operate. Funding may be needed for research and development, equipment, service facilities, marketing, raw materials and labor. Months may pass before products have been produced and have actually made their way to distribution points for sale to the consumer. Retail businesses may generally require less start-up money than manufacturing businesses. Nevertheless, initial costs of inventory, advertising, leased space and labor for a retail store may quickly mount up. Service businesses may require almost no initial capital, if the product is personal services (such as consulting services) and if you do not start off with elaborate offices or expensive advertising. If, on the other hand, your service business is a motel or restaurant, start-up and ongoing costs will be significantly higher. Compared with manufacturing, retail and service businesses, mail-order businesses may require the least amount of capital. Initial expenses will be travel and telephone costs to select products to offer, the design and printing of a catalog and/or advertising, mailing list purchase, postage and answering-service costs. You may be able to structure a mail-order business so that you do not have to pay for the products you are offering for sale until the orders are placed and payment is received.

The comparisons of the preceding paragraph are very broad generalizations. It is impossible to draw broad conclusions about business financing requirements that will be accurate in every instance because of the countless variables involved. Two people who each start a company to manufacture exactly the same product could end up with very different start-up and operational costs. Perhaps one will arrange to handle all facets of manufacturing through the company, while the other will reduce start-up and operational costs by subcontracting a portion of the functions.

A well-thought-out business plan is necessary to adequately determine the capital requirements of the business you are considering. As discussed more fully in the chapter on business planning ("Planning Your Itinerary"), be realistic in your plan. Do not be overly optimistic with projections that will leave you short of cash. Certain rules of thumb are applicable in most businesses. For instance, do not expect to make a profit the first year. In fact, do not expect to break even (i.e. have sales equal to expenses) for at least six months.

The Small Business Administration and most public libraries have books containing financial statistics for various types of businesses. We have listed some of these books under "Financial Information" in Exhibit C. The United States Department of Commerce also publishes a wealth of financial and other statistical information about various industries and business categories. Such statistics may also be available through trade associations for the industry that you are investigating. These studies and statistics may be very helpful to you in assessing your options.

### Level of Expertise

As discussed earlier, experience is an invaluable asset when starting a business. It is possible to build a successful business in a field in which you have no experience; however, your level of risk will be higher than it would if you were experienced. If you are not experienced in your chosen business, you may reduce the risk level in a variety of ways. For example, you could find a business partner or key employee with the necessary expertise; arrange for an apprenticeship with a company similar to the one you wish to form; purchase a franchise, allowing you to benefit from the experience of the franchisor; or hire a consultant experienced in your desired line of business.

If you want to manufacture a product but do not have any experience in manufacturing, you should plan to have a business partner or key employee who does have the experience, or you should consider an alternative, such as licensing, which will be described in more detail below. The risks in manufacturing are high enough without adding the risk of lack of experience. Service businesses normally require a high level of expertise and may have barriers to entry such as training and licensing requirements – health care professionals, lawyers and real estate brokers, for example. Although prior experience would enhance one's potential for success in the retail and mail-order fields, these areas generally require less prior experience than manufacturing or service businesses.

### *Risk Comfort-Level*

What level of risk do you, personally, feel comfortable assuming? What do you stand to lose if your business does not succeed? What risks are associated with the opportunity that you are considering? How can you reduce or control those risks?

Some of the risks associated with a start-up operation are the risks of: (1) development (Can you develop your idea into a product?); (2) production (Will you be able to economically produce your product?); (3) marketing (Once produced, can you effectively market your product?); (4) management (If you can sell the product, can you sell it at a profit?); (5) growth (Can you effectively manage the growth of the business?).

The enjoyment of your entrepreneurial journey will depend, to a large extent, on whether or not you feel comfortable with the risks that you have assumed. Risk comfort-levels vary from person to person. Risk can give an "edge" that motivates and inspires action. Many people, however, reach a point where risk ceases to motivate and, instead, becomes debilitating due to the level of stress that it generates.

Only you know what your risk comfort-level is, so only you will know whether a particular business opportunity may be structured to fit within that comfort-level.

## *Financial Return*

What are your expectations concerning the amount of money you will make from your business? Will the business you are considering meet your expectations?

Of course, potential financial return is only one of many factors to consider in deciding whether to start a particular business. You may be much better off operating a business you truly love, but which pays you only $30,000 per year, rather than tolerating one that makes you miserable, but pays in the six figures. There is a certain heartfelt appeal to such stories as the high-powered wall street executive who turns his back on the glamour, financial reward and stress to move to the mountains to start a cross-country ski lodge and live the "good life." Financial return is, however, an important factor to consider in deciding whether to pursue a particular business.

Given the preceding discussion regarding the time, money and experience requirements for manufacturing, you may wonder why anyone chooses to start a manufacturing business. The risk of loss in the event of failure is very high. The reason why manufacturing is attractive to some entrepreneurs is that it often proves true the cliché, "the greater the risk, the greater the potential return."

Because such large sums are usually required for manufacturing, the founder(s) of the company will often end up giving up more ownership in the business to investors than would be required for other industries. If you start with 100% ownership of a manufacturing business, by the time you reach the public-offering stage of financing, you may be lucky to own 20% of your company. Of course, 20% of a company with millions in assets and annual sales is a substantial equity interest.

The risk/return formula usually applies to service and retail businesses, as well. A service or retail business requiring more investment and lead time generally has greater potential reward than a business requiring less of an investment and lead time. If it does not, you should re-evaluate your plans before proceeding. For example, starting a computer services company or a large department store would require more money and risk than starting a consulting business or a small retail shop. The projected return on the investment should also be significantly higher, or else the level of investment may not be justified.

Every business has some limits on its income and profit potential. What are the limitations on the amount of money that may be generated by the business opportunity you are considering? Are the limits acceptable or would you prefer to pursue an idea with fewer or different limits? Some factors affecting the income and profit potential of a business include geographic market area, whether or not income is tied to hours expended, the number of customers that may be serviced within a set period of time, capital requirements and manufacturing or distribution limitations.

Often, the broader the potential geographic market for a business, the greater the potential for expanding sales and increasing profits. The geographic market area is usually more limited for retail and some service businesses than for manufacturing or mail-order businesses. A business such as a clothing boutique or a restaurant draws its customers primarily from people who live or work within a convenient commuting distance of the business location. On the other hand, the customer base for a manufacturer, mail-order company, and some service businesses (such as consultants in specialized areas) may have no geographic limits. The customer base could be worldwide.

Although mail order, like manufacturing, is able to reach a wide geographic market, it may have other limitations. Some people will not purchase from a catalog or brochure. They may prefer to go into a retail store, examine the product that they are purchasing and then take the product home immediately upon paying for it. Therefore, mail order must often offer products that are unique or that are not readily available through retail establishments. Another crucial element for the success of a mail-order business is gaining access to an up-to-date mailing list of the best target market for the product.

Some service-oriented businesses (such as doctors, lawyers, plumbers, carpenters, or consultants) are restricted in potential income because compensation is based primarily upon an hourly fee. The amount of that hourly fee is usually limited by what the market is willing to pay for the particular type of service. Therefore, income is limited by the number of hours in a day and the number of customers who are willing and interested in paying for services at the rate charged. An independent provider of services charging hourly fees for services only makes money when he or she is working and does not generate income when on vacation or unable to work because of illness. Other businesses, such as retail, manufacturing, and mail-order companies, are not subject to this particular restriction. Nevertheless, depending upon the hourly fee charged, you may still be able to make more money in such a service business than in other areas that are of interest.

The income of a service business such as a hotel or restaurant is restricted by the number of rooms or tables and the number of customers who frequent the establishment. Of course, a business of this type may overcome such restrictions by expanding its facility or opening additional facilities, but such expansion may require considerable additional financial investment.

There are some factors that affect the level of return on investment, no matter what type of business. You must have a product that is priced right for its target market, so that people will buy it, and you must have an effective distribution system, so that the product will reach the optimal target market. Also, unless your product is a standard product or service that people use and then continue to have a need for (such as soap, food and other consumables), you may reach a point where the market has become saturated with your product. At that point, it may no longer be economical to market the product. If you are producing such a product, it is best to recognize the market-saturation limitation and to arrange to sell the company and realize your return on investment before reaching the saturation point.

We have addressed limitations on financial return in this section solely for the purpose of helping to realistically assess the financial potential of a business. Such a realistic assessment prior to starting a business helps avoid unpleasant surprises once the business has begun. Once a limitation has been perceived, it often may be side-stepped or eliminated by creative solutions.

## Alternatives to Creating a Business "From Scratch"

❖   Some entrepreneurial alternatives include licensing, purchasing a franchise or distributorship, acquiring an existing business or becoming an intrapreneur.

❖   Countless other alternatives are waiting to be developed or discovered by the creative mind looking for fulfillment.

When analyzing business options, realize that there are many variations and permutations for you to consider, allowing you incredible flexibility to choose a venture that meets your desires and needs. If you prefer not to start a completely new business "from scratch," you could consider other alternatives, such as licensing, purchasing a franchise or distributorship, acquiring an existing business or becoming an intrapreneur. These are not all your options, however. Countless other alternatives are waiting to be developed or discovered by the creative mind looking for fulfillment.

### *Licensing*

Licensing is an option you should consider if you have created a product or product idea that you want to mass-market but you, yourself, do not want to assume the risk and responsibility of manufacturing and distributing the product. Under a licensing arrangement, you would grant another party (the "licensee") the right to produce and market the prod-

uct. In exchange for granting this right, you would receive a percentage of income (a "royalty") from the
sale of the licensed product.

Another situation in which licensing might
prove beneficial is if you want to manufacture
and/or distribute your product yourself, but you want
the product to bear a trademark that was developed
by someone else. For instance, maybe you have created a children's toy that you want to market under
the trademark of one of the Disney characters. You
could enter into a license agreement with the owner
of the established trademark that grants you the right
to use the trademark on your product. In exchange
for this right, you would pay the licensor a royalty on
income generated from the sale of your product. This
arrangement may greatly accelerate and increase your
market penetration by giving you instant name
recognition, access to an existing sales force, participation in trade shows, discount advertising rates or
other valuable marketing assets that you creatively
negotiate with the licensor of the trademark.

Licensing arrangements abound in such industries as electronics, apparel and software. Obviously,
some products are more suitable for licensing than
others.

Of course, licensing is not risk-free. The risk that
someone may try to imitate your idea always exists. If
you license another party to produce and distribute
your product, you would be well-advised to first take
every precaution to protect the intellectual property
rights associated with your product, such as patent,
copyright and trademark rights.

Another risk is that the company you select as
licensee will not aggressively or successfully produce
and market your product. To avoid getting stuck with
a nonaggressive licensee, your license agreement

should contain measurable performance standards, or the right to license others to produce and distribute the product, or both.

## Franchises/Distributorships

Franchises and distributorships are independently-owned businesses. They afford the business owner much of the independence of the entrepreneur, while often having less risk than other types of entrepreneurial ventures. Although franchises and distributorships are different from each other in many ways, they also have many similarities.

The owner of a franchised business (the "franchisee") enters into a franchise agreement with the owner of the franchise system (the "franchisor"). Under the agreement, the franchisor grants the franchisee the licensed right to use the name of the franchise, provides the franchisee assistance in the start-up and ongoing operation of the franchise, and often coordinates national or regional advertising programs to promote the franchise. The franchisee pays the franchisor an up-front fee and ongoing royalties and fees for the continuing right to participate in the franchise system.

Under a typical distributorship arrangement, the owner of a distributorship has an agreement with the producer of a product to market the product to retail establishments. Some distributors purchase the products for resale to retailers at a markup. Other distributors serve more as sales agents, taking orders for the products and receiving a sales commission. Sometimes a business that is called a distributorship may actually be a franchise, according to the legal definition of the term.

Franchises and distributorships may have a lower risk than other types of entrepreneurial ventures because the franchisor or grantor of the distributorship (both of which we'll call the "grantor") wants to see the franchisee or distributor (both of which we'll call the "grantee") succeed. Therefore, the grantor is usually willing to provide assistance to help ensure success. The grantor wants a 100% success rate among grantees because the more successful and profitable the grantee, the more successful and profitable the grantor.

To say that the risk is lower for these types of ventures does not mean they are risk-free. There are risks – that the grantor may become bankrupt or go out of business, leaving the grantee without products to sell; that the grantor will not provide the assistance promised; that the location selected for the grantee's business does not have the market-draw that was anticipated; that the grantor will try to terminate the rights of the grantee to continue in business. Generally, however, the risks are easier to assess and control than with other types of entrepreneurial ventures.

If your goal is to own your own business and make a decent salary, but with a more controlled risk-level, then franchising or distributorships may be the type of businesses you should consider. You may not become "filthy rich" with this kind of business (you will be sharing your profits with someone else), but you will be your own boss and will experience the freedom of being an entrepreneur, within the constraints imposed by your franchisor or grantor of distributorship rights.

## Acquiring an Existing Business

One option for owning and operating your own business is to acquire an existing business. This option offers the advantages of avoiding the lead time associated with start-up operations; knowing exactly what sort of income, expenses and return to expect; and acquiring an existing customer base and a known image. This option may not always seem to provide the opportunity for the same degree of creative expression that is experienced when building a business "from scratch." Nevertheless, there are still many opportunities to be creative through modifying the image, expanding the customer base or improving operations.

When you acquire a business, you have the option of continuing its current identity and methods of operation or restructuring the business to meet your own goals. If your idea is to start a manufacturing operation or a restaurant, for example, and you know of existing operations that are available for acquisition at a reasonable price, you might be able to save time and money by acquiring those operations and then modifying them to suit your purposes.

Deciding whether to acquire an existing business rather than starting one's own business requires a thorough analysis of the pros and cons of your particular situation. Is the asking price for the business reasonable? For the same amount of money, would you be better off building your own new image and acquiring new equipment or a different location? How long would it take to build the same customer base if you started the business "from scratch?"

If you choose to acquire an existing operation, be sure to conduct a detailed review of all aspects of the business before acquiring it. The purpose of such a review should be: (1) to protect yourself from liabilities incurred by the current owners; (2) to gain a clear concept of all factors affecting the market demand for the product (Is this, for example, a restaurant frequented by a fickle "fad-following" crowd that has now moved on to a new and different chic place?); (3) to learn of any impending, large, out-of-the-ordinary expenditures that need to be made; and (4) to gain a clear understanding of all the pluses and minuses associated with operating this particular business.

It is often preferable to acquire the assets of the business, including the trade name, rather than to acquire the corporate stock or other equity interest of the current owner of the business. An asset acquisition helps protect against unknown liabilities that may have been previously incurred by the corporation or other entity that currently owns the business.

To recite and analyze all of the factors to consider in acquiring a business would require a separate book. We mention the option here merely to acknowledge that it is an option available to the aspiring entrepreneur. If you choose this route, proceed with caution. In the experience of the authors, the most successful acquisitions are usually accomplished by knowledgeable, adequately-financed businesspeople who comprehend the numerous tax and financial maneuverings available for acquiring and financially restructuring the target company.

### *Becoming an Intrapreneur*

Are you a creative person with the entrepreneurial spirit working for someone else and feeling that you are not in a position to leave your salaried position? Do you, perhaps, have financial obligations

– home, car, children, credit card debts, etc. – that make you uncomfortable with the risk of starting your own business? Do you feel the drive to be an entrepreneur but find that you have not uncovered the business idea that feels like the right one for you? Are you an inventive person who loves to dream up and design products but who would not enjoy administering a business?

Don't despair! You can still find ways to express your entrepreneurial drive within traditional employment relationships. More and more companies are recognizing the value of discovering and promoting the development of the intrapreneur within their own ranks. A company would be terrifically short-sighted if it did not promote the creative spirit of its employees. That's how new and better products and operational procedures are born.

Many exceptionally creative people have chosen to generate and develop their ideas within companies owned by someone else. Inventors, for example, often find that the best application of their talents is to become an employee of a company with the resources to finance the production and marketing of the products they create.

Look for ways to bring new ideas to your company, and look for the supervisory people who are willing to listen to and promote such ideas. As you build a reputation as an intrapreneur, you should be able to realize financial rewards from your efforts, either through promotions, or participation in profits tied to your ideas, or both. If the company you are currently working for does not encourage your intrapreneurial development, there are countless others that would welcome your talents, so explore!

# *Travel Partners*

❖ If you build the business with cofounders, choose good business partners and not just friends.

❖ Focus on the talents needed to make the business succeed and assure yourself that the person you are considering as a cofounder has strengths in those areas.

❖ For the protection of all parties, arrange for an attorney to prepare the necessary employment and equity-participation documents before the parties commence their cofounding relationship.

Do you want to make your business journey alone, or do you want travel partners to make the journey with you? Starting and operating a business calls for a variety of skills and a commitment of significant time and resources. Working with appropriate cofounders may create results in a fraction of the time that would be required if you were working alone. On the other hand, entering a business venture with cofounders who are not a good match may double or triple the time required to achieve results and may, in fact, lead to the failure of the business endeavor.

How do you know whether or not a person would be an appropriate cofounder? There is no failsafe formula for making that determination, but there are certain guidelines to follow.

Focus on the talents needed to make the business succeed and assure yourself that the person you are considering as a cofounder has strengths in those areas. It is often tempting to select friends as cofounders because you like them, they are already known to you and they are probably very supportive of your idea. Nevertheless, try to avoid the security blanket of choosing friends, especially inexperienced friends, as cofounders. It is amazing to witness the rationalizations that some entrepreneurs have concerning the imagined talents of friends – be aware of this trap. Choose people who will be good business partners and not just friends. This is not to say that you should never select friends as cofounders. Sometimes, such an arrangement may work very well. Just be sure that you are selecting your cofounder based on talent and business considerations and not just for convenience or emotional reasons.

As you research your business idea and, later, as you are raising capital, you will meet many individuals with knowledge and talents that can help your business. During this period, you may realize the need to supplement your business idea with additional talent.

The priorities placed on talents that you are seeking in potential cofounders – such as sales, engineering, marketing, operations, or financing skills – will vary based on your own talents and the sophistication and complexity of your business. Your fundraising activities often will help place priorities on the talents you are seeking. If you have difficulty raising money, you may observe a trend in the reasons for rejection by investors. Frequently, investors may think you have a great business idea but may believe that the talent to implement the idea is lacking.

Once the needed talent is identified and the person possessing such talent is located, it is often necessary to make that person a cofounder for economic reasons. Normally, talented individuals are accustomed to good pay. An embryonic business may not have the cash flow to meet the salary expectations of a talented individual but may offer other off-setting opportunities to reap the financial rewards of participation in the business. Offering equity and cofounding responsibility to the person with the talents you are seeking may be just the needed incentive to secure a commitment from that person to join your team. A talented professional's willingness to forego a high salary to potentially make more through equity participation in your business will lend tremendous credibility to your business venture in the eyes of potential investors.

For the protection of all parties, arrange for an experienced attorney to prepare the necessary employment and equity-participation documents before the parties commence their cofounding relationship. These documents should describe the rights and responsibilities of all parties and should specify what will happen if the relationship does not work out as planned or if additional equity participants are brought into the company. It is much better to spell out such expectations as fully as possible at the beginning of a relationship than to try to resolve misunderstandings after the fact.

## Summary Tour

If you are trying to select a business idea to pursue, the following will guide that decision:

### THE BASICS

* Choose a business that is a good match with your personality and interests.

* Choose a business that has market and profit potential equal to or greater than your financial expectations.

* Choose a business with a very specific market niche.

### DISCOVERING BUSINESS IDEAS

* If you want to start a business but you don't have a specific idea in mind, the best approach is to develop a specific frame of mind. Tell your subconscious mind that you want a business idea and then use every possible opportunity to watch for ideas.

### ANALYZING THE OPTIONS

* Assess your own time availability, financial resources, expertise, risk comfort-level and financial expectations. Then choose a business that is the best match with your resources and expectations.

- Just as venture capital companies analyze hundreds of deals before committing money to a particular one, you are, in a sense, a venture capitalist with your own time, money and energy to invest. You should analyze your options carefully before committing yourself to one.

## ALTERNATIVES TO CREATING A BUSINESS "FROM SCRATCH"

- Some entrepreneurial alternatives include licensing, purchasing a franchise or distributorship, acquiring an existing business or becoming an intrapreneur.

- Countless other alternatives are waiting to be developed or discovered by the creative mind looking for fulfillment.

## TRAVEL PARTNERS

- If you build the business with cofounders, choose good business partners and not just friends.

- Focus on the talents needed to make the business succeed and assure yourself that the person you are considering as a cofounder has strengths in those areas.

- For the protection of all parties, arrange for an attorney to prepare the necessary employment and equity-participation documents before the parties commence their cofounding relationship.

# Chapter 3

# Planning Your Itinerary
## (The Business Plan)

## Chapter Destination

*Will you wander aimlessly toward your destination or will you proceed with a sense of direction? This chapter examines the value of plotting your course before you proceed. It explores the 'hows and whys' of preparing and presenting a successful business plan. Although the chapter provides some hints for writing a business plan, the primary focus is on how to use the plan, rather than how to write it.*

## Purpose of the Business Plan

❖ A business plan and its financial projections are useful for:

- Determining for yourself if the business idea will be worth the time and resources required to develop the business.

- Assessing additional resources that you may need to make the business successful.

- Selling your business idea to sources of financing and to key staff.

- Monitoring performance.

- Projecting cash-flow needs.

There is really no one "right way" to start a business. It is possible to start your entrepreneurial journey without a business plan. Just as it is possible for you to start a journey in your car from a starting point in Florida to a destination point in Alaska without ever looking at a map, you can start your entrepreneurial journey toward your business destination without ever thinking about the route you are going to take. However, just as a map allows you to pick the best, most direct highways and helps avoid major travel delays for your automobile journey, so will a business plan make your business journey more direct and easy.

How do you know that your business idea will be worth the time and resources required to develop it? You could spend months or years building a business and then realize too late that the business idea never had the potential for providing the kind of income and return that you had hoped. Before starting your business, why not use the business-planning process to analyze your idea from every angle to satisfy yourself that it has the potential for fulfilling your financial expectations?

The business plan not only helps project financial return, but also can help you anticipate additional resources (people, money, etc.) that you may need to successfully develop the business in the least amount of time. The earlier you can spot the need for these resources, the more lead time you will have for finding them. This, in turn, will make your business development process much smoother and easier.

Preparing a well-thought-out business plan is particularly important if you are one of the fortunate creators not only of a new product or service but also of a whole new industry or a major subset of an existing industry. To be in this position is the absolute epitome of an entrepreneurial journey. In such a case, however, you are entering uncharted waters. It is vital to research and plan your steps carefully by analyzing other more mature industries, getting feedback from customers and incorporating what you learn into a detailed business plan.

One of the greatest values of the business plan is its use for selling your business idea to sources of financing and to key staff. Potential sources of financing want evidence that you have a clear plan for how to make an operational business out of your idea. They also want to know what kind of return to expect on their investment. A properly prepared business plan answers these questions and concerns. A well-developed business plan is also invaluable for demonstrating to potential key staff members that you have a clear plan for developing a company on which they can risk their futures.

Most investors realize that the potential success of going from an idea to profitable business rests on the abilities of a solid management team. Therefore, they will generally insist that a company have an experienced accountant or chief financial officer prior to funding or shortly thereafter, depending on the size and complexity of the deal. It is preferable to have at least some of the key members of the management team on staff, or at least committed to the project, as early as possible in the planning phase of the business. Identifying and assembling the management team is part of the entrepreneur's initial research into the feasibility of his or her idea. If quality people are not interested in joining the management team, analyze why – is it your presentation and terms, some flaw in your idea, or just a lack of a good match between the idea and the people you have approached?

If the management team is identified in advance, then they can and should help put together the business plan. This will enable you and your prospective team to work together before full commitment to the project. It will also let all parties thoroughly analyze the deal and will lend much greater credibility to the business plan. A successful business is much more easily created if a compatible team is in place working together to build the business.

A business plan should not be something that collects dust in a back drawer of your desk once you have used it to secure your financing and your business team. It should be a reference resource for your business that you consult on a regular basis to help determine the extent to which you are meeting your target goals and projections. The business plan will help you keep track of the big picture of your business goals and direction, when you are in danger of getting buried in detail and when you need to regain a broad perspective for making wise business decisions. It is best to review your business plan in detail at least annually, revising it to reflect changes in the direction of your company.

The projections in your business plan may prove invaluable for anticipating the cash-flow needs of your business. A properly developed plan has a detailed cash-flow projection that can be used to predict the financial needs of the business in advance. This allows the entrepreneur to effectively manage that often rare commodity called "cash."

The plan should contain accurate assumptions concerning: (1) the time required for collecting accounts receivable (COD sales may actually average 7-10 days for collection and "net 30" may really average 45-60 days for collection.); (2) credit terms and limits with vendors (Will prepay or COD be required or will "net 30" or other terms be granted? If terms are granted, what is the dollar limit?); and (3) inventory turnover (How much inventory must you stock in relation to sales?). The successful entrepreneur will quickly learn how to apply these assumptions to calculate cash-flow needs, even if the projections in the plan turn out to be inaccurate.

A common mistake made by entrepreneurs is underestimating the cash requirements of operating the business. They may, for example, naively assume that a vendor will immediately grant 30-day payment terms with sufficiently-high credit limits. In fact, it usually takes several months to achieve 30-day terms with adequate credit limits. A vendor's requirement of payment within 30 days with a $5,000 credit limit for a business that uses $10,000 per month of the vendor's product is, effectively, a requirement of payment within 15 days. By preparing a plan and thinking through all of these issues, you will gain a realistic idea of the cash-flow requirements of your business. You will learn when and to what extent additional financing will be needed.

Another common error is to falsely assume that inventory levels and sales rates will be equal and that, consequently, cash out to vendors and cash in from customers will be fairly comparable. Unfortunately, businesses generally must acquire or manufacture all or at least a portion of their inventory in advance to meet reasonable delivery times to customers. Therefore, they may be required to pay for at least a portion of their inventory in advance of receiving payments from customers. It is important to understand the acquisition and manufacturing lead times of your product(s) and the delivery demands of your customers. Then you can reasonably forecast inventory turnover and its effect on your cash flow.

The following example helps illustrate the importance of timing when budgeting the cash flow for a project. Assume you have decided to invest $50,000 in an advertising campaign that is projected to generate around $200,000 in profits. The bottom line of this simple budget would clearly tell you that it is a worthwhile investment. However, you must look at the cash flow for the project, as well as the bottom line of projected profits, to discover the full impact of the campaign on your operations. The advertising expenses will probably need to be paid before the campaign even runs. Then there will be a delay of perhaps two to four months before sales are derived from the campaign. There may be an even further delay before those sales are converted to cash. That means that you may be forced to wait months before sales start bringing in cash to cover your up-front $50,000 expense. If you have not anticipated and planned to cover this collection delay, the potentially profitable campaign may become a major, short-term cash-drain on the company. The cash-flow crunch could then have a devastating domino effect. The cash shortage could prevent you from obtaining necessary inventory to fill the orders generated from the campaign. This could cause one or both of two negative results: (1) you could generate bad will with customers because of late shipments or (2) you may realize fewer sales and lower profits (less cash) than planned. Once you realistically look at the flow of cash out and cash in, you can anticipate and avoid these potential problems. By planning ahead, you can prepare to find additional financing to cover the cash-flow crunch or decide to spend less than originally planned. Just remember what Harold Geneen, former chairman of ITT once said: "The only irreparable mistake in business is to run out of cash."

When projecting cash flow, include a cash cushion or reserve for product or delivery delays, business downturns, bad debts or unanticipated occurrences.

## *Preparation and Presentation of the Business Plan*

❖ Use the plan both as a planning tool and a selling tool.

❖ Keep the plan simple – cover the important points but without too much detail.

❖ Let the plan create a visual image of your business – include graphics and pictures as well as words and numbers.

❖ Research and draft the plan yourself, but unless you have the time and expertise, hire professionals to complete it or review it (preferably, future members of your management team).

❖ Stress your strong points, but also identify weak points while providing solutions for them.

❖    **Practice presenting your plan.**

The business plan should not only be a planning tool, but it should also be a selling tool for your company. There is no one correct form for a business plan. There are, however, major points that most financing sources look for in a plan. These should be included in your plan if you want it to be given serious consideration.

For best results, start the business plan with a one- or two-page summary that gives potential investors an overview of the products or services being offered by the business, the location, the target market, what distinguishes your business from competitors' businesses, the key management staff, financial highlights, your projected development schedule and statements of why you believe your business will be successful. The rest of the business plan should then go into detail regarding each of these points and the planned growth of the business. For your reference, a sample business plan outline is provided in Appendix B.

For help in completing the detailed portions of the plan, there are many resources (many of which are listed in Appendix C) that will provide sample business plans and financial and operational information regarding specific categories of businesses. The Small Business Administration, the United States Department of Commerce, book stores, entrepreneurial organizations, trade associations and most public libraries have a wealth of business and statistical information useful for preparing business plans. Also, most venture capital firms, accountants, or other financial service professionals have sample business plans that they are willing to share with clients and prospects.

Keep the plan simple. The plan should be long enough to cover salient facts about your business but should not be so long as to be burdensome. It may be useful to have a concise plan of from 20-40 pages and to also have a separately-bound volume containing additional detail and background information for the benefit of investors who wish to see further explanations of points covered in your plan.

Make your business plan visually convey the image you want to project. Include marketing literature, charts and graphs. Make it colorful! A picture or sketch of your product and plant will say at a glance what you could spend pages trying to describe in words. A sample of your marketing literature will serve as an actual demonstration of how you plan to sell your product. In addition to numbers showing three to five years of sales projections, profits and cost of sales, include a bar chart or line graph depicting the growth you project in those areas. The visual image of an upward graph will stick in the mind of the business plan reader much longer than the lists of numbers.

Include a chart that lists or graphs milestones for the development of your business such as the following:

- Obtain Seed Capital                    March 7
- Develop prototype                      March 8-May 30
- Complete financing for
  production of first 500 units          June 30
- Produce first 500 units                July 1-August 1
- Test market                            August 1 - Sept. 1
- Develop sales and marketing
  literature                             Sept. 1 - Sept. 30

Such a chart will give a concise summary of the steps required to implement your business and the projected timetable. It will also serve as a checklist of accomplishments, which may not only be personally reassuring but also a very effective sales tool to use with potential investors. The milestones could be highlighted in a simple format, such as the one in the preceding paragraph, or could be presented more graphically, using flow charts, calendars or some other pictorial representation.

The plan should state facts and should not lie or exaggerate. It should, however, be written in a manner that generates interest and excitement among investors. When preparing a business plan, entrepreneurs often err by either being too conservative or too liberal in projections. If they are too conservative, the projections may not generate enough excitement to interest investors. If, on the other hand, they are too liberal, investors may suspect that the projections are wild numbers that are much too high to be believable. Don't be too conservative, but don't be so aggressive in your projections that you can't possibly deliver the projected results.

It is best to be more conservative in your projections for the first six months to one year. Then be more aggressive in your projections for years two through five, which are further down the road, giving you more time to get there. What you do not want to do is show that you are going to have a fabulous first six months, then not meet your projections. This would leave you open to questions and pressures from investors or your bank. If you need to show a big first year, be prudent and show the greater portion of those sales and earnings coming in the last six months of that first year. Give yourself a fighting chance to get started. You want to structure the business so that you do not put any more pressure on yourself than necessary. You want to keep control of the business in your own eyes and in the eyes of your investors.

Most financing sources prefer business plans that have projections of from three to five years. Of course, projections for any period beyond a couple of weeks or months are often "pie in the sky." Nevertheless, preparing projections should force you to realistically analyze the potential market size for your business. Then your sales projections should correspond to and be derived from your market analysis. Projections by no means guarantee success, but they do allow you to estimate your profitability if you do succeed.

The first year's projections should be by month and should have a detailed breakdown of income and expenses with supporting schedules. The next two years should be by quarter, with summaries of projected income and expenses. Subsequent years should be annualized and presented in a very summary manner.

It is important to support your first year's sales  projections with well-researched, realistic assumptions. Analyze market share, number of units of each product that must be sold, cost of sales, product mix, pricing, etc. This is your reality check – do it. You may not need to include in the business plan, itself, the detailed analysis you used to arrive at your projections. The details should, however, be readily available to support the plan when questions arise. It is a very embarrassing and potentially damaging situation to be asked by a prospective investor, "How did you come up with your sales data?" or "Upon what did you base your sales and cost of sales?" and then not be able to answer. It is amazing how many people fail to properly support their projections with adequate analysis or "fudge" the numbers to achieve a desired bottom line that they cannot support with their analysis.

One area where experienced professional consultants can provide invaluable assistance to the entrepreneur is in assisting with the preparation of the business plan, particularly the market analysis and projections sections. To invest a little money in obtaining qualified assistance in preparing these portions of the business plan could be one of the key decisions an entrepreneur makes. If you do decide to hire professionals to assist with the business plan, just remember that you are the person who will be responsible for marketing your business idea and implementing the plan. Therefore, it is essential that you stay intimately involved in the preparation of the plan. You should probably do some of the initial research and prepare a first draft of the plan yourself, even if it is not in standard business plan format. Then, use your consultants to analyze your research, gather more supporting data, help develop the assumptions and projections, and add form and polish to the plan. You must work closely with your consultants throughout this process, actively participating in the writing and forecasting. You should feel satisfied that the assumptions on which the numbers are based are realistic and accurate. Do not be afraid to question your consultants or to make them explain and defend their interpretations of the projections. You must be 100% comfortable with everything that is represented in your plan.

An excellent way to verify the accuracy of your projections is to compare them with the financial statements and operating history of an existing business that is similar to the one you are starting. If you know of a publicly-held company that is in a line of business similar to your planned business, you can find extensive financial and other information available to the public about such company. You can review such information yourself in the offices of the United States Securities and Exchange Commission ("SEC") or contact one of the companies in the business of making copies of such SEC records for the public (for a fee, of course). You might also contact a brokerage house or the company, itself, to request an Annual Report and the most recent Form 10-K and/or 10-Q. The 10-K and 10-Q Forms are annual (K) and quarterly (Q) financial reports that the SEC requires public companies to file. If you call companies directly and ask for their investor relations or marketing departments, they will often send additional promotional literature as well. You should by no means copy the data you receive or in any other way violate other companies' copyrights. Just use the information to confirm in your own mind if your projections are realistic.

Remember, when writing your plan, your business will have strong points and weak points. Stress your strong points, but also identify weak points while providing solutions for them. Do not try to fluff over weak points – confront them directly with real solutions. An advantage of using this approach is that it forces the resolution of potential problems before they become problems. It also reassures potential investors that the business has been well-thought-through. Furthermore, identifying weak points may help avoid future allegations by investors that they were misled or that information was withheld that would have caused them not to invest in the business.

Once you have completed your business plan, it is critical to practice your presentation of the plan before your first real meeting. If possible, arrange for your business consultants, management team or other trusted advisors to review and critique your presentation.

When raising money for a business, there are many federal and state laws that will affect the manner in which you proceed. Failure to comply with these laws may result in severe civil or criminal penalties. There are, for example, restrictions on the number and type of investors that you may approach, the type of disclosures that you may make about your business, and the manner in which you approach potential investors. There are also government filing requirements which vary depending upon the nature of the offering. These may apply to your fund-raising activities. Before approaching or distributing any printed material to prospective investors, you should consult with legal counsel qualified and experienced in securities laws for guidance as to the proper method of proceeding. Such counsel should provide appropriate disclaimer language to include in your business plan in order to avoid possible securities law violations.

## *Summary Tour*

### PURPOSE OF THE BUSINESS PLAN

A business plan and its financial projections are useful for:

- Determining for yourself if the business idea will be worth the time and resources required to develop the business.

- Assessing additional resources that you may need to make the business successful.

- Selling your business idea to sources of financing and to key staff.

- Monitoring performance.

- Projecting cash-flow needs.

### PREPARATION AND PRESENTATION OF THE BUSINESS PLAN

- Use the plan both as a planning tool and a selling tool.

- Keep the plan simple – cover the important points but without too much detail.

- Let the plan create a visual image of your business – include graphics and pictures as well as words and numbers.

- Research and draft the plan yourself, but unless you have the time and expertise, hire professionals to complete it or review it (preferably, future members of your management team).

- Stress your strong points, but also identify weak points while providing solutions for them.

- Practice presenting your plan.

# Chapter 4

## Designing the Tour Package
### (Marketing Strategies)

### Chapter Destination

*What sort of tour package (marketing strategies) will you select for reaching your destination? You may have the world's greatest business idea, but unless you know how to effectively market that idea, you will not have a successful business. This chapter walks you through the design of a marketing strategy, from selecting the market niche and creating the product image to pricing and promoting the product.*

## Marketing Philosophy and Strategy

❖ **The fundamental principle of marketing is to always focus on the customer.**

❖ **Sacrificing customer service and support for short-term profit or other goals can lead to short-term businesses.**

❖ Adopt a clear, concise, company philosophy that emphasizes marketing and the importance of the customer. Then make sure that every company employee knows and practices that philosophy.

❖ Marketing is a complete system of interacting business activities designed to plan, price, promote, and distribute want-satisfying products and services to present and potential customers.

❖ A marketing strategy consists of five major components: (1) Selecting the target market; (2) Creating the image for the product to appeal to the target market; (3) Pricing the product; (4) Promoting the product; and (5) Selling the product.

Marketing is one of the single most important factors affecting the success or failure of a business. The world's greatest product or service will not give rise to a successful business until marketing lets the world know the product or service exists and convinces customers to buy it. Once customers have discovered the product or service, the role of marketing then shifts to keeping the customers satisfied and coming back for more. The goal of marketing is to bring customers to the product or service and then to keep them there.

The fundamental principle of marketing is to always focus on the customer. Of course, the bottom line goal of most businesses is to make as much money as possible, but to reach that goal, the focus must be on the customer. In essence, customer want-satisfaction is the economic and social justification of a company's existence. If no customers are buying your product or service, then you have no business. Therefore, all company planning, policies, and operations should be oriented toward the customer. What does the customer want or need and how may your product or service best be presented to meet that want or need? All company activities – planning, production, marketing, sales, finance, administration – should be devoted first to determining what the customer's wants are and then to satisfying those wants while still making a reasonable profit.

Although the importance of the customer seems obvious, there are countless, every-day examples of businesses that have forgotten this basic marketing principle. How many times have you been a customer of a company that treated you as though they were doing you a favor, instead of acknowledging that you were doing them a favor by being their customer? Perhaps you have shopped in a store where the clerks arrogantly treated you as though you were fortunate that they let you walk through the doors of their establishment. Perhaps you have been the client of a "prestigious" law firm or accounting firm where the lawyers or accountants made you feel that they were doing you a favor by accepting your business or meeting your time deadlines. How many times have you called a company for service or support for a product, only to be given the run-around or a promise of a call back that never comes? How many times have you ordered a product, based on a promised delivery date, only to have to keep calling to see why it is late? An incredible number of companies give lip service to the importance of their customers and to keeping them as customers forever; however, far too few companies operate their businesses so that this actually occurs.

Forgetting the importance of the customer is one of the biggest marketing errors that any company can make. Sacrificing customer service and support for short-term profit or other goals can lead to short-term businesses. How can you keep your business from making this mistake? One of the best ways is to adopt a clear, concise, company philosophy that emphasizes marketing and the importance of the customer. Then make sure that every company employee knows and practices that philosophy. A concise company philosophy provides a cornerstone for building an image. It keeps everyone, owners and employees alike, focused on what is important to the company, serves as the basis for making decisions, and guides the way in which customers are treated. Having a guiding company philosophy becomes even more important as your company grows and there are more and more employees in direct contact with your customers.

The benefit of adopting a marketing-oriented company philosophy may be seen by looking at some of the large and successful companies. For example, IBM and Nordstrom Department Store are known for their commitment to customer service. German automobile companies are known for their engineering. McDonald's Restaurants are known for their cleanliness, efficiency and consistency. How have such large businesses established those reputations? They have had firm, clear, company policies and philosophies known to every employee and enforced by every manager of every part of the business. Their philosophies are designed to satisfy customers. This, in turn, has attracted and kept customers and has been a major cause of the growth and success of these companies.

Once you have defined your marketing philosophy, then you will be ready to develop your marketing strategy. The importance of a marketing strategy is evidenced by the fact that in many industries, the number-one-selling product is often not the best product. In such instances, the reason the product is the top seller is not because of its inherent qualities as compared with those of its competitors. It is the top seller because of the success of its marketing program.

Successful companies have come to realize the importance of developing a clear and effective marketing strategy prior to launching a product. Many large companies now routinely spend millions of dollars to research and develop a marketing strategy before introducing a new product. The entrepreneur is usually not in a position to spend such large amounts of money to develop a marketing strategy but should at least spend time thinking through the same marketing issues that the large companies consider when developing new products.

Before forming a marketing strategy, you may ask, what is "marketing" and what is a "marketing strategy?" Marketing is a complete system of interacting business activities designed to plan, price, promote, and distribute want-satisfying products and services to present and potential customers. A marketing strategy consists of five major components: (1) Selecting the target market; (2) Creating the image for the product to appeal to the target market; (3) Pricing the product; (4) Promoting the product; and (5) Selling the product. Each component is important to the success of the marketing effort.

The remainder of this chapter will introduce you to the basics of the first four components of a marketing strategy. The fifth component, sales, is discussed separately in chapter 6, "Moving on Down the

Road." Because we are dealing just with the basics and because of the importance of marketing to the success of the company, we strongly recommend that you read at least one or two books devoted exclusively to marketing theories and strategies before launching your business.

Although we may speak in terms of "products" in this chapter, the same marketing principles apply to services and intangible, as well as tangible, products.

## Selecting the Target Market

❖   Determine the best target market for your product – which segments of the population will most want to buy your product and will be the type of customers that you most want to serve.

❖   Be a "niche player" – define the market niche and then sell as many product units as possible to each customer within that niche.

❖   Test market your product on a limited scale to gather information and feedback before going into full production.

What is the best target market for your product – which segments of the population will most want to buy your  product and will be the type of customers that you most want to serve?  This is one of the most important marketing decisions you will make and one that will be the driving force behind most of your other marketing decisions.

Determining the target market includes consideration of questions such as the following:  To what age group do you want to sell? Will you be selling primarily to males, females, or both? Do you want to limit your marketing efforts to a local area or do you want to market on a regional or national basis? Do the people in your target market occupy a particular social status or possess certain personality traits to which you wish to appeal?

Maybe your target market is "baby boomers," or maybe even the "yuppie" subset of the baby boomers. Maybe it is teenagers, the elderly, people who visit the beach, microcomputer users, athletes, people earning over $50,000 annually, people who live in cities or those who live in the country, businesses with 1 to 15 employees located within a 25-mile radius of your office, or corporations with over $5 million per year in sales.

No matter which target market you choose, it is important that the target market be as focused as possible. Be a "niche player" – define the market niche and then sell as many product units as possible to each customer within that niche. By marketing to a narrow market niche, it is easier to establish an image and reputation and gain market domination than when marketing to a broad target market. Once a person within that niche becomes a customer, it is then possible to return to that customer to sell additional units of the product or family of products, enhancements, or similar types of products. It is much less costly to sell to the same customer three different times than it is to sell one time to three different customers.

The more defined your target market niche, the easier it will be to develop an effective image for your product to appeal to customers within that niche. If you try to appeal to all segments of the population, you may end up with an image that is so nebulous and dispersed that it does not effectively appeal to any particular market segment. On the other hand, your niche should not be so narrowly defined that there are not enough customers in it to generate a profitable sales base.

There is no exact science to selecting the characteristics and size of a market niche. Often refining the definition of the niche is a result of trial and error. There are some "rules of thumb" for selecting market niches, but these should be used as guides, only, and not as hard and fast rules. For example, one formula for determining the appropriate size for a market niche is to select one where a 15 – 50% share of that market provides a satisfactory return to the entrepreneur and investors. The important point is to have a clear concept of the identity and characteristics of your market niche, Then be open to adjusting the definition of that niche if necessary.

Selecting a particular niche does not mean that you must confine yourself to just that one niche. It is usually possible to continually expand your target market by pursuing additional niches. Often this process begins naturally, without a conscious decision by the entrepreneur. Although such entry into new niches may occur without being planned, the successful entrepreneur quickly sees the trend and takes appropriate action to capitalize on it.

Through clever positioning, it is possible to find successful market niches even in what appear to be overcrowded marketplaces. The key is to narrowly define the market niche and then position yourself by creating the image as the expert and undisputed leader in that niche.

For example, the microcomputer manufacturing industry rapidly became what appeared to be an overcrowded and saturated field. Compaq Computer, however, was able to enter that industry and achieve one billion dollars in annual sales faster than any other American company in history. It did so by targeting a niche with a demand that had not yet been met and by establishing itself as the leader in meeting that demand. The demand was for a high-quality, transportable computer. Once Compaq established its base by filling that specialized niche, it then had the reputation and resources to expand its product line to include a full range of high-quality microcomputer hardware products.

Another way of positioning a product for success is to find an industry that may be strong nationally but that may be weak in certain geographic areas. Perhaps the current leaders in the industry have not focused on a particular geographic market because it is difficult to truck the product to that market, or it is too costly to hire sales people there. Perhaps the industry leader has not penetrated a particular geographic market because in the ten-year expansion plan of the company, it is year four and that geographic area will not be developed until year eight. Whatever the reason, the big companies are not paying attention to the geographic area. This leaves an opening for a smaller company to come in, focus on the market, and become the market leader in that geographic area.

Often, the large markets that appear closed to competition because of market dominance by a few giants in the industry are the best places to look for niches. If the market is large, the industry giants may become complacent or caught up in fierce competition for the national market. They may miss many profitable, smaller niches.

If your product has the potential for appealing to diverse segments of the population, the best approach may be to go after one of your best target market niches first. Then, after you have established a presence in that market niche, repackage the product and use different promotional techniques aimed at different target markets rather than using the same approach for all target market niches.

A prime example of repackaging a product to appeal to different market segments is toothpaste. Toothpaste manufacturers take what is basically one product and then they put it in different containers and use different promotional tactics to sell that same product to different market segments. They make it striped and put it in squirt cans to appeal to children. They put it in traditional tubes and tout its fluoride protection or tartar removal to appeal to adults. They add different flavors to appeal to different tastes. In essence, they are creating different images for the same product to appeal to different market niches.

If you use the tactic of repackaging to appeal to different market niches, just be careful not to undermine your existing market. Once consumers decide they need or want a particular type of goods or services, they then purchase a specific product or service because of a perceived image that has been created around the product and/or company. When reaching out to a new niche, first analyze the success of your existing niche and image. Avoid taking any action that might discredit or diminish your existing market position unless the new market is larger and more profitable.

Products that are extremely successful within their niche often gain demand from other niches and become "mainstream," appealing to a broad cross section. Apparel manufacturers, for example, often introduce a product line with a narrow market-niche appeal and then take it to the mainstream consumer.

When this occurs, as it did with Levi's jeans, Reebok shoes, and expensive sunglasses, the entrepreneur can achieve success beyond his or her wildest dreams. These products were generally designed and marketed to a specific niche, but, because the timing, market, product, customer, and production were all right, the success literally spilled over into new markets.

Whatever target market you pinpoint for your product, it is important to test market your product on a limited scale to gather information and feedback on pricing, packaging, production capabilities, and sales and marketing strategies before going into full production. Test marketing the concept or product at the earliest possible date is critical. It is very expensive to develop an inappropriate or ineffective marketing or sales strategy. Errors in marketing judgment may cause unnecessary commitments of time and money to the wrong sales and marketing literature, hiring the wrong people, selecting the wrong product packaging, leasing inappropriate office space, producing unsaleable inventory, or securing inappropriate advertising. Test marketing helps correct errors in judgment before making substantial financial commitments. If you have chosen the wrong fork in the road, test marketing helps you realize that error before you have traveled too far down the road to turn back.

## Creating the Image

❖ **Once a target-market niche has been identified, the goal is to create the image for the product to most effectively appeal to consumers within that niche.**

❖   **The first step in creating the image is to understand the needs, desires and personality attributes of the target-market consumer.**

Once a target-market niche has been identified, the goal is to create the image for the product to most effectively appeal to consumers within that niche. The first step in achieving this goal is to understand the needs, desires and personality attributes of the target-market consumer. Then all decisions concerning the image should be geared toward meeting those needs and appealing to those desires and attributes.

There are some products that, through image alone, have become tremendous marketing successes – for example, the "Pet Rock." Who would ever have thought that people would pay several dollars for a rock? There was nothing special about the rock, but with a clever concept, name, and container, it was packaged in such a way that an incredible number were sold.

It is often possible to vary the image of a product or service, with minimal added cost, so that it appeals to different target-market niches. It may also be possible to redesign a product for different purposes, so that the same individual will purchase more than one. These techniques may substantially increase sales with very little added cost, thereby enhancing both gross income and net profits.

The example of repackaging toothpaste for different markets was given earlier in this chapter. Another example is sodas. Most soda manufacturers market not only their standard soda, but also a diet version, caffeine-free version, fruit version and various combinations thereof – all variations of the same product and each aimed at a different target market.

Other examples of products that have applied the multiple packaging principle are wet suits and athletic shoes. The same wet suit product may be marketed as a "dive suit," "jet-ski suit," "surfing suit," or "winter suit" for skiers. Maybe there are slight variations in each named product – different colors, styles or thicknesses – so that a person who surfs, dives and snow skis simply must own three different wet suits: a spring suit that is brightly colored with short legs for surfing; a winter suit that is thicker and that has long legs; and a dive suit with special, subtle colors that do not attract the attention of sharks. As for athletic shoes, there was a time in the past when you could use the same pair of shoes for tennis, basketball, running and other athletic activities. Now, if you are going to a resort for your vacation, you need an entire suitcase just to carry shoes for the occasion – tennis shoes, golf shoes, walking shoes and running shoes, to name a few.

The remainder of this section will discuss some of the elements affecting the image of a product.

### *Value of the Product*

❖   **No matter what product or service you are selling, the heart of the image created for that product or service is its value.**

❖   **An excellent image-creating tactic is to give the customer more than expected.**

No matter what product or service you are selling, the heart of the image created for that product or service is its value. The value is based on a variety of real and perceived characteristics, including product quality, performance, price, competitive standing and source of distribution.

Consumers generally realize that within a product category the competing products will range widely in value due to variations in quality, price and the ability to meet the needs of the consumer. Consumers evaluate the characteristics of the competing products and the ability of each to meet their needs and desires. Then they choose the product that they consider to be the best value. Most buyers try to select products that have the best quality and performance for the price. Obviously, the more costly the product, the more elaborate the customer's evaluation process. The decision between competing brands of a supermarket product may take seconds, while the choice of a new automobile may take days or weeks.

In some industries, the **quality of service** provided in connection with a product is as important in determining the value of the product as is the quality of the product, itself. This is particularly true for electronic products. The fact that a computer hardware product or a software package is the most advanced, powerful product on the market does not mean much if there is not a responsive company standing behind the product, ready to provide repair and maintenance services in a timely manner or answers to questions about using the product.

For this reason, the source through which the product is purchased often significantly influences the customer's perception of value. A buyer shopping for a computer or facsimile machine for business use might be especially concerned about the ability to obtain product support services and quick repairs. He or she might choose to pay a premium price to purchase from a conveniently-located retailer with qualified, responsive, support personnel. On the other hand, a purchaser of a computer or facsimile machine for home use might be less concerned about the technical support for the product and might, therefore, choose to purchase the same product from a discount or mail-order establishment.

Recognizing the potential impact of the distribution source on the perceived value of the product, some product manufacturers go to great lengths to select and restrict the distributors and retailers who may sell their products. This is true both for products, such as computers, which require servicing and knowledgeable sales forces, and products which do not require servicing but which depend upon the retailer to project a particular image, such as high-priced designer clothing.

On the other hand, manufacturers of products which do not depend very heavily on the point of sale to convey value for the product may try for the fastest and widest distribution for the product. They may allow sales through discount and mail-order establishments as well as through higher-priced, retail establishments.

A customer's perception of a product's value is influenced not only by actual product characteristics, such as features, price, and performance, but also by customer expectations. Sometimes those expectations result from advertisements and promotions for the product or from knowledge of the value of other products bearing the same brand name. Other times the expectations are simply based on the customer's experience with or knowledge of other competing products.

An excellent image-creating tactic is to give the customer more than expected. People have become accustomed to receiving minimal quality and service for their money. Therefore, "going the extra mile" and giving more than expected can work wonders in creating a positive image and generating exceptional good will for a product.

This tactic is particularly successful in service-oriented businesses. For example, Domino's Pizza quickly captured market share by guaranteeing delivery within a specified time period. The guarantee was backed by a reduction in price in the event of late delivery.

Another example of going the extra mile is Nordstrom, a major west coast department store that decided to move into an east coast area saturated with other large, well-known, department stores. Nordstrom made an impact and created an image that quickly drew customers. Its salespeople are trained to give exceptional service and live, classical music is performed on a grand piano in the store. Naturally, a customer would prefer to shop in a store with an elegant, but comfortable, ambiance where sales clerks are smiling and eager to offer assistance rather than shop where the clerks are indifferent and act as though the customers should do everything for themselves.

### *Name, Logo and Slogan*

❖   The more of an image you can create with the name of the product, the more easily you will be able to reach your target market.

❖   The name, logo and slogans constitute valuable assets of your company. They should be carefully selected and adequately protected.

The name for a product may be a very powerful marketing tool. The name can create an immediate image for the product – its use, qualities and the type of customer to whom it is geared. The more of an image you can create with your name, the more easily you will be able to reach your target market. This is particularly important when you have a new product and limited financial resources to promote it.

Just as the name may promote a particular product image, so may logos and promotional slogans that are selected for the product create an image. Your logo and slogan may impart an image of seriousness, humor, luxury, economy, creativity, traditionalism – any image that is appropriate to the target market that you are trying to reach.

There are a number of different strategies for selecting a name. The strategy used will depend upon the type of product or service you are promoting and the type of image you wish to project. Some of the more common strategies for selecting names are described below.

## Descriptive Names

Probably the most common approach for selecting a name is to choose one that in some way describes the product or service that the company is selling. Examples include:

Digital Equipment Corporation
Burger King
International Business Machines
Computerland
Toys-R-Us
Body Glove

Some of the companies in the preceding example, such as "Toys-R-Us" and "Body Glove," exercised some marketing flair in the names selected, while others, such as "Computerland" and "International Business Machines," were descriptive in a more serious vein. The type of product or service you are selling will influence the amount of flair and marketing creativity that should be used in the name. For instance, it may be more appropriate and clever, in the eyes of the consuming public, to use flair in the selection of a name for a toy store than in the selection of a name for a company that sells office machines to businesses.

In the case of the above examples, the names originally selected by Digital Equipment Corporation and International Business Machines were descriptive of the products sold. The companies and their products then became so well-known that abbreviated forms of the names, "DEC" and "IBM," came to be used as much as or more than the original names.

## Coined Descriptive Names

Closely related to the descriptive strategy for name selection is the creation of a name by combining all or parts of descriptive "buzzwords" from an industry or words descriptive of the product. Examples of this approach are:

| | |
|---|---|
| dBASE II | Microsoft |
| Lotus 1-2-3 | WordPerfect |
| Micropro | Turbo Pascal |

Used properly, this strategy for name selection may create a distinctive and memorable identity and image for a product. Names such as those above were vaguely descriptive, while full of marketing flair. The products with which they were associated were new, but the use of buzzwords and descriptive phrases imparted a sense of establishment, history and technical quality that contributed to the quick acceptance and success of the products.

### Symbolic Names

Sometimes a name is not overtly descriptive of the product or service offered but is meant to be symbolic in some way. Often such names are designed to elicit feelings of expansiveness, security, or confidence. For example:

| | |
|---|---|
| Safeway Stores | General Motors |
| Federal Express | Standard Brands |
| American Motors | Union Oil |

### Founder Names

A common strategy for name selection is to name the product or business after the founder. While providing a basis for distinguishing the product or service from those offered by other parties, this strategy usually does little, in and of itself, to create an image for the product. When the names "Ford" and "DuPont" were first used, they did not automatically elicit a particular image. It was only through association of those names with a particular caliber and type of product that the names eventually became associated with an image.

Of course, there are some industries in which the use of the founder's name is the accepted strategy for name selection. Those names are then accepted as being indicators of a particular quality or value of goods. This is especially true in the fashion industry, where names such as Calvin Klein, Liz Claiborne, and Christian Dior call to mind a particular image and are associated with specific target markets.

## "Off the Wall" Names

One of the riskiest approaches to selecting a name, but an approach that may create tremendous marketing strength if it is successful, is to choose a name that is "off the wall" – a name that bears no rational relationship to the product or service being marketed, or that is extreme and elicits shock, interest, amusement, curiosity, or some other emotional response. The following names fall within this category:

|  |  |
|---|---|
| Apple Computer | The Beatles |
| Egghead Software | The Grateful Dead |

Unique names, such as the preceding, may provide a marketing edge, being both memorable and promotable. Some of the initial objectives of marketing are to create interest in the product or service and to develop name recognition. "Off the wall" names may accomplish both of these goals. A unique name that generates interest may quickly open doors for free media coverage for a product. It is also likely to stand out in the minds of the target market customers and may give a competitive edge over other products. An added benefit to an "off the wall" name is that if the name and the product are successfully received by the target market, consumers of the product often develop an especially strong identification with or devotion to the product.

Two of the names from the preceding example are associated with entertainment, an industry that lends itself well to the selection of "off the wall," memorable names. The other two examples are associated with the computer industry, an industry that, until recent years, might have been considered so serious and conservative that names like "Apple Computer" and "Egghead Software" would be presumed to doom a product to failure. The reason these names were effective was that the target market for consumers of computer products changed. The old target market was composed of large businesses that could afford very expensive computer systems. Serious business names had been chosen for products designed to be sold to this target market. As less-expensive personal computers were developed, the target market changed to smaller businesses and individuals who wanted computers for their own personal use. Companies designing products for this new target market realized that many of the initial consumers from this market would be people who were daring enough to try new and unique products. They also realized that, in order to appeal to a broad base of consumers, they would have to overcome the "techno-fear" of many prospective consumers who had not used computers before. Their products would need a more friendly, inviting image than had been associated with earlier computer products designed solely for big businesses. Sensing these characteristics of the new target-market consumers, the producers of the new computer products often chose names that implied uniqueness or that associated friendly, non-intimidating characteristics with their very technical products. This marketing tactic was extremely successful in attracting and winning over the targeted consumers.

## Nebulous Names

Some names have little or no descriptive qualities and may not elicit any particular reaction in the listener. Names such as "Exxon," "Signet," "Westin" or "Federated" would not automatically imply that they are associated with a particular type of product. Sometimes such names are selected for the very reason that they do not create a particular image or because the sound of the name, due to the use of certain letter combinations, creates a subtle response in the listener. Companies choosing such nebulous names usually do not rely on the names, themselves, to create an image in the public mind. Rather, they use their advertising and other marketing resources (which are often substantial) to create the desired image.

## Protecting Names, Logos and Slogans

The name, logo and slogans constitute valuable assets of your company. They should be carefully selected and adequately protected. You will need to assure yourself that the names, logos or slogans you have selected are not confusingly similar to those being used by companies marketing competing products or services. Otherwise, you may end up embroiled in costly suits filed by such companies claiming that you are infringing their trademarks or service marks. If you infringe someone else's marks, you may be forced to endure the expense and confusion of changing your name, logo or slogan. You may also be required to pay damages to the owner of the marks that you have infringed.

In addition to satisfying yourself that you are not infringing someone else's marks, you should also take appropriate steps to protect the trademark or service mark rights in the names, logos and slogans you select from infringement by others. Federal and state registration of marks is often advisable, particularly if the business will be marketing or expanding beyond a local geographic area.

In "The Entrepreneur's Business Start-up Checklist" (Appendix A), we have suggested ways to assure yourself that you are not infringing someone else's marks and ways to protect the marks you have selected.

### *Physical Appearance*

❖ **One of the most important aspects of image creation is the physical appearance of a product – the way it looks, the way it is displayed, and the way it is "wrapped" for delivery to the consumer.**

One of the most important aspects of image creation is the physical appearance of a product – the way it looks, the way it is displayed, and the way it is "wrapped" for delivery to the consumer. Most consumers form immediate impressions of quality and value based upon the way a product looks. Those impressions are often difficult, if not impossible, to change. Therefore, it is extremely important to ensure that the desired impressions are elicited.

A meal served with artful garnishes on gold-rimmed, fine china by waiters in tuxedos creates an entirely different image than exactly the same food ladled onto chipped china from giant kettles behind the serving counter by waiters in soiled aprons. The food is the same, but the image (and consequently the clientele and the price) are at opposite poles.

Appearance is important not only for tangible products, but also for intangible products and services. A law office waiting room with elegant, oak-panelled walls, oriental rugs, fresh cut flowers, plush leather chairs and no clutter creates an entirely different image for a client than a law office waiting room with tattered vinyl chairs, metal filing cabinets and papers strewn about in disorderly stacks. A client may be inclined to run from the latter office rather than risk getting lost in the disorder. The lawyer practicing in the latter setting may be more skilled than the lawyer practicing in the more orderly office. Nevertheless, clients would probably perceive that the services of the lawyer in the disorderly setting were worth less because of the appearance of the office.

Packaging applies to people as well as products, as evidenced by the "Dress for Success" movement that flowered in the 1970's. A consultant dressed in crisp, tailored, business attire for a first meeting with a client will, more than likely, be perceived as more knowledgeable and competent than a consultant who attends such a meeting dressed in ill-fitting casual-wear that looks as though it has been slept in.

If you are selling a tangible product, in addition to considering the actual appearance of the product, it is very important to control, as much as possible, how the product is displayed at the point of sale. Guidance on how and where to display the product for resale to the consumer must be given to resellers of a product. Sales of the product will not be maximized if the product is stored in an out-of-the-way location or is displayed in an inferior fashion compared to a competing product.

For example, assume you are manufacturing a software product for distribution through existing retail channels. The distributors and retailers have typically set up their facilities to ship and merchandise products in fairly standard ways, based on input from and experience with the manufacturers of their existing product lines. The manufacturer of a new product must understand the distribution channel so that the product can be shipped and then displayed in the desired manner. Do you want your software product displayed alongside your competitor so that the buyer can easily compare features and, as a result of your product's superior features and price, select your product? Do you want your product off the shelf and away from the other products so that it will be seen first and its clever packaging will sell it before the buyer even gets to the competing product? Maybe you do not have a direct competitor and you are selling the retailer on a new product concept that will use previously unused space within the store, thereby offering the potential to increase sales per square foot. If you offer a display device with your product, can the distributor ship it? The list of questions and possibilities is limitless, as are the answers for the resourceful entrepreneur. The key is to make sure you research and understand the selling channels so that you can make the most effective use of them.

In some industries, display methods make a particularly strong  statement about image. For example, supermarkets have seized this concept to draw particular types of customers. For years, supermarkets all had more or less the same appearance. Then, some new supermarkets sprang up with a low-overhead, warehouse-price image. The stores had bare-bones, display shelves and often kept crates of products stacked above the display cases, creating the impression of high volume and no frills. Prices charged in such stores were usually considerably less than the those charged by the traditional supermarket. Customers, who realized that the products were the same in both stores, began to flock to the warehouse-type stores to save money. Pretty soon, the traditional supermarkets began installing bare-bones shelves with crates of goods stacked above them and advertising "warehouse prices."

At the same time that a supermarket chain might be converting some of its locations to the warehouse image, however, that same chain might be opening other stores with a more up-scale, luxurious image. These stores are designed to appeal to the consumer who prefers shopping in more refined surroundings where unique grocery items are sold, along with standard items, and who is less concerned with saving money.

Product containers, themselves, play an important marketing role. Containers are often designed to catch the eye and create a lasting image. Sometimes containers play a marketing role from a functional standpoint, as well as from the standpoint of appearance. Think how often you have shook and poked to get ketchup to pour out of a newly-opened, thin-necked glass bottle onto your french fries. Why did it take decades for someone to produce ketchup packaged in a plastic, squeezable bottle?

The way the product is delivered to the customer is another packaging technique that creates an impression. A gift shop that places all purchased items in attractive boxes with pretty ribbon and gold seals may attract more repeat customers than a gift shop selling the same items that shoves purchases into brown paper bags. Customers of a financial-planning firm may feel that they are receiving extra value if they are presented financial plans in attractive binders with their names stamped in gold rather

than being given financial plans that are stapled together in the corner with no cover.

The examples of the importance of product appearance to marketing are endless. The point is that
very serious consideration should be given to every
aspect of the appearance of your product and business. Appearance will influence the types of customers you will draw and what they are willing to
pay for whatever you are selling.

## *Location*

❖ **Be sure the location you choose conforms with
   the image you are trying to project, gives the
   highest possible visibility, and makes sense from
   a cost standpoint.**

You frequently hear the quote that the reasons
why a particular business or investment has succeeded are "Location, Location, and Location." Location of a business is important for a variety of reasons, some of which are related to marketing and
others of which are related to other considerations,
such as cost.

The reasons why location is important to a
manufacturing business are different from the reasons why it is important to retail or service businesses, such as a gift shop or restaurant. A manufacturing company may base a location decision on such
considerations as the distance from points of distribution, proximity to shipping sources, cost of land,
availability of qualified labor, and tax rates. On the
other hand, retail and service businesses, while considering some of the same factors, also take into account the way in which the location enhances or coordinates with the image they wish to impart. A bou-

tique that sells high-priced designer clothes must be located in an area that is accessible to and frequented by high-income customers and that imparts the ambiance that would appeal to such customers.

Visibility of a location is also crucial to many retail and service businesses, particularly those that rely heavily on street traffic and drop-in customers. A donut shop needs to be in a location that many people pass by, particularly in the morning. Donuts are often an impulse purchase and not something that a consumer would go out of his or her way to buy. An elegant restaurant, on the other hand, has more customers who plan their visits rather than customers who just happen to stop by, so location in an area with heavy traffic may not be as important as it would for a donut shop.

Although image and visibility are very important for the selection of a location, equally important is whether or not the cost of the location makes sense. The potential for business generated because of the location must be in line with the cost.

When selecting a location, just be sure that the one you choose conforms with the image you are trying to project, gives the highest possible visibility, and makes sense from a cost standpoint.

## Pricing

❖   The price must be sufficient to cover all the expenses and overhead for producing and selling the product, plus a markup for profit.

❖   The price should be in line with the image that you wish to project for the product, the expectations of the target market and the prices of competing products.

❖ Expect that there will be price adjustments once you have test-marketed the product and have a better idea of the demand for the product and the expense of producing it.

❖ Besides the per-unit price, other pricing issues to consider when marketing a product include minimum order requirements, payment terms and discount policies.

One very critical element of marketing a product is its price. Price influences the demand for the product and contributes to the product's image, as well as determining the profitability of the business.

There are numerous factors to consider in pricing a product. First of all, there is the obvious principle that the price must be sufficient to cover all the expenses and overhead for producing and selling the product, plus a mark-up for profit.

This principle may seem obvious. All too often, however, an entrepreneur prices a product or service only to discover later that the price doesn't cover the costs of producing the product or providing the service. Perhaps certain costs of doing business were overlooked or not anticipated in setting the price, or maybe the projected sales volume used to calculate cost per unit was erroneous. The result is that each unit sells at a loss. It is important to keep accurate records of all business costs and to periodically evaluate whether or not the prices charged are covering such costs. Otherwise the entrepreneur may never make any money from the business.

Beyond this basic premise, there are other factors to consider in determining price. The price should be in line with the image that you wish to project for the product and the expectations of the target market. The price should also be in line with prices of competing products. If the product is designed to be marketed to economy-minded or volume buyers, then there will be little room for marking the price up beyond what is needed to cover expenses and overhead plus a narrow profit. On the other hand, if the product is one for which the public expects to pay a premium and volume-purchase discounts are not involved, then the established price and the profit per unit should be much higher.

An example of this latter principle is a company that produced paintings at a cost of $2.50 per painting. The company tried selling the paintings door-to-door for $5.00 each, a 100% mark-up. No one wanted to buy the paintings at this price. The company owners then changed their marketing strategy. People value art, so they had to charge enough for the consumer to perceive the art had value. It would not be unusual for someone to spend $50 for a painting. Therefore, the company adopted the strategy of saying to the consumer: "Here is our regular $49.95 artwork. We're running a special promotion during which time we will sell it to you for $19.95." With this strategy, the company could not make enough paintings to meet the demand for the paintings. The new pricing strategy placed a value on the artwork but was low enough that people would make a spontaneous decision to purchase.

Pricing a product is often an inexact process. You may find that the price that seemed sufficient to cover overhead, in the beginning, later becomes insufficient as you expand your marketing efforts to new geographic areas or wider markets or as the costs of supplies or labor increase. It is usually easier to lower a price than it is to raise it, so it is usually a better policy to set a price that may seem on the high side in the beginning. In any case, you should expect that there will be price adjustments once you have test-marketed the product and have a better idea of the demand for the product and the expense of producing it. Typically, a company manufacturing or selling a successful tangible product will be able to lower the price over time. This is often true because, as the demand for the product builds, the product may be produced at lower cost. As larger quantities of the product are produced, the manufacturing cost per unit is usually lower. Further cost savings may result from discounts for purchasing larger volumes of the raw materials used to manufacture the product.

Besides the per-unit price, there are other pricing issues to consider when marketing a product, such as discount policies, minimum order requirements, and payment terms.

It is important to encourage viable buyers to purchase in quantity and not just sample the product line. This will enable larger production runs, which will  lower the per unit cost of each product and lead to higher profit margins. As this happens, the most successful entrepreneurs operate efficiently enough to increase their own profits, while passing a portion of the savings on to the customer. Establishing discount policies for larger volume purchases is a pricing strategy that may encourage larger purchases of the product. For example, you might tell the customer, "We can discount beyond our published prices if you order the product in quantity with one delivery date. We only do four production runs per year. If you do not commit to purchase now, we may not be able to fill your next order for several months. That would be unfortunate because you know this is going to be a very popular product and we have committed to advertise extensively, etc."

Another way to encourage volume purchases is to adopt a policy that a product will not be sold to resellers of the product in quantities below a certain number. It is less costly to deal with five resellers who each purchase 100 units of a product than it is to deal with 100 resellers who each purchase 5 units. Also, the more units a reseller purchases, the more attention the reseller will give to reselling that inventory.

As for payment terms, there are a variety of cash and credit structures that may be established. The more costly the product, the more important the terms of payment are to the saleability of the product. The more unique the product and the greater the demand for the product, the less crucial the payment terms are to the saleability of the product.

If you are selling a product to a distributor or retailer for resale to the target-market consumer, then requiring a substantial up-front payment from such distributor or retailer will help from two standpoints. First, the down payment may be used immediately to fund additional production of the product or may be expended on promised promotional activities. Second, the fact that the reseller has made a substantial up-front financial commitment will give the reseller added incentive to resell the product as quickly as possible to generate cash to pay for it. The reseller will then encourage the sales staff to prominently display and push the sale of the product.

Requiring substantial up-front payments is usually only successful if the product is in demand, properly priced, well-packaged, and supported with a good promotional campaign. A distributor or retailer may stock hundreds or thousands of different products. It is, therefore, vital to somehow cause these resellers to focus attention on your product through effective marketing. The more the entrepreneur learns about marketing through reading, experience, or advice from others skilled in marketing, the more likely he or she will find the best approach for selling his or her product to resellers as well as to the target consumer.

## Promoting the Product

❖ **Advertising should broadcast an image of the product that appeals to the target-market needs and desires, which in turn leads to the sale of the product.**

❖ **There are many low-cost, even free, avenues available to advertise your product.**

❖ **Analyze which methods of advertising are most likely to reach your target market and select approaches that are likely to get the greatest response for the money spent.**

❖ **Test market and periodically re-evaluate your advertising methods to ensure that you are using the most effective approaches for your product.**

Once a market niche is identified and the product's image has been packaged, the last remaining marketing step is to promote the product – to expose the product's image to the target market customer.

Advertising is the primary method of such promotion. Sales techniques and distribution channels, which are also part of the promotional process, will be discussed in chapter 6, "Moving on Down the Road."

The world's greatest product could end up just sitting on the shelf unless there is an effective advertising campaign to let the world know that the product exists. Advertising should broadcast an image of the product that appeals to the target-market needs and desires, which in turn leads to the sale of the product.

Advertising comes in many forms and serves many different purposes. Basically, the type and content of advertising that will be used to market a product will depend upon the image that is to be projected and the distribution channels that have been selected. It is not the intent of this book to guide you through all of the components of a successful advertising campaign. Rather, our purpose is to make you aware of the necessity of advertising and to open your eyes to the fact that there are many low-cost, even free, avenues available to advertise your product. Entire books have been written about ways to generate free and low-cost publicity and ways to plan an advertising campaign. These are worth consulting to stimulate ideas for your own advertising approach. You should also consider consulting an advertising firm that is knowledgeable about advertising your particular type of product and that is known for creative solutions to advertising challenges.

Local newspapers, television shows and radio stations are always looking for a story. If you have a unique product or service or can think of an unusual promotional tactic, you may be able to obtain such media coverage for your product. Also, almost every industry has trade magazines that need and want material for stories. Approach the target media with an idea for a story on you or your product. Be sure to plan your presentation and give them a "hook" or an angle to write about that will catch the attention of their readers.

Before contacting a publication with your story, examine several issues of that publication to become familiar with its style and focus and to decide in which section of the publication you wish to be featured. If the publication is a newspaper, do you want to appear in the style, business or local news section? How could your story best be presented to attract interest and readership? Many publications devote stories and news to their largest advertisers. At least initially, your budget probably will not permit you to fit within that category, so creative "hooks" may be your best hope. The "hook" may be based on the uniqueness of the product or service, itself; or the story behind the idea; or a promotional gimmick; or any number of other angles.

When considering advertising that costs money, analyze which methods of advertising are most likely to reach your target market and select approaches that are likely to get the greatest response for the money spent. If you select an expensive radio or television advertising spot, for example, you will be hitting only a small part of your target market and only for the short time the advertisement is aired. You may, however, appeal to enough of your target-market customers and generate enough sales to justify that expense. On the other hand, you may find that your money would be better spent on direct mailers to your targeted customers or some other less expensive approach that is likely to reach more of your target market or provide a more lasting impact. The timing of advertisements is also a critical element for ensuring the most return for your advertising dollar. For example, an advertisement that is run on the radio at 4:00 a.m. is not likely to reach the ears of many prospective consumers.

Consider a "test marketing" approach for your advertising. Try several different approaches and see which one generates the highest response rate and units sold for the dollars spent. Key-coding responses to advertisements is an excellent way to keep track of where your customers are coming from. For example, you might advertise in a newspaper, giving a particular code number in the response address, such as "Department A-200," while advertising in a particular magazine with a different response code, such as "Department B-106." Then you keep track of how many orders are addressed to each of the key-coded addresses to determine which of your advertisements are generating the most responses. Advertising tactics should be periodically re-evaluated to ensure that you are using the most effective approaches for your product.

## Summary Tour

### MARKETING PHILOSOPHY AND STRATEGY

* The fundamental principle of marketing is to always focus on the customer.

* Sacrificing customer service and support for short-term profit or other goals can lead to short-term businesses.

* Adopt a clear, concise, company philosophy that emphasizes marketing and the importance of the customer. Then make sure that every company employee knows and practices that philosophy.

* Marketing is a complete system of interacting business activities designed to plan, price, promote, and distribute want-satisfying products and services to present and potential customers.

* A marketing strategy consists of five major components: (1) Selecting the target market; (2) Creating the image for the product to appeal to the target market; (3) Pricing the product; (4) Promoting the product; and (5) Selling the product.

### SELECTING THE TARGET MARKET

* Determine the best target market for your product – which segments of the population will most want to buy your product and will be the type of customers that you most want to serve.

- Be a "niche player" – define the market niche and then sell as many product units as possible to each customer within that niche.

- Test market your product on a limited scale to gather information and feedback before going into full production.

### CREATING THE IMAGE

- Once a target-market niche has been identified, the goal is to create the image for the product to most effectively appeal to consumers within that niche.

- The first step in creating the image is to understand the needs, desires and personality attributes of the target-market consumer.

### *Value of the Product*

- No matter what product or service you are selling, the heart of the image created for that product or service is its value.

- An excellent image-creating tactic is to give the customer more than expected.

### *Name, Logo and Slogan*

- The more of an image you can create with the name of the product, the more easily you will be able to reach your target market.

- The name, logo and slogans constitute valuable assets of your company. They should be carefully selected and adequately protected.

## Physical Appearance

- One of the most important aspects of image creation is the physical appearance of a product – the way it looks, the way it is displayed, and the way it is "wrapped" for delivery to the consumer.

## Location

- Be sure the location you choose conforms with the image you are trying to project, gives the highest possible visibility, and makes sense from a cost standpoint.

## PRICING

- The price must be sufficient to cover all the expenses and overhead for producing and selling the product, plus a markup for profit.

- The price should be in line with the image that you wish to project for the product, the expectations of the target market and the prices of competing products.

- Expect that there will be price adjustments once you have test-marketed the product and have a better idea of the demand for the product and the expense of producing it.

- Besides the per-unit price, other pricing issues to consider when marketing a product include minimum order requirements, payment terms and discount policies.

## PROMOTING THE PRODUCT

- Advertising should broadcast an image of the product that appeals to the target-market needs and desires, which in turn leads to the sale of the product.

- There are many low-cost, even free, avenues available to advertise your product.

- Analyze which methods of advertising are most likely to reach your target market and select approaches that are likely to get the greatest response for the money spent.

- Test market and periodically re-evaluate your advertising methods to ensure that you are using the most effective approaches for your product.

# Chapter 5

# Financing the Expedition
## (Financing the Business)

## Chapter Destination

*One of the biggest roadblocks for most people to overcome in their entrepreneurial journey is financing the business. How do you come up with enough money to start the business and how do you raise the money to keep it going once it is started? This chapter examines financing strategies, phases and sources.*

## Financing Strategies

❖ **There is no secret road to successfully raising money.**

❖ **The key to succeeding in your quest for funds, no matter what route you choose, is to understand and apply some basic strategies, then be creative and persistent.**

There is no secret road to successfully raising money, especially for start-up businesses. Luck and timing can play as much of a role in the financing process as do planning, preparation and the value of your business idea. The key to succeeding in your quest for funds, no matter what route you choose, is to understand and apply some basic strategies (such as the ones discussed in this section), then be creative and persistent.

Except in extremely unusual circumstances, remember that the money won't just fall in your lap. You have to aggressively pursue it. Just because you have one of the world's most creative concepts or you have held a prestigious position in your line of business doesn't mean that the money will magnetically attach itself to you. It might, but don't count on it. More than likely, you will have to present your idea to countless prospects before you find appropriate financing. The more you understand this, the less likely you will be discouraged by the financing process.

Raising money involves many stages – developing the business plan, determining what types of financing are required and when, deciding which potential investors to approach, approaching those sources and structuring the deal. For the purposes of this chapter, we'll assume that your business plan is complete (at least for now, as it should be continually revised) and we'll focus on the strategies and steps to take to complete the remaining steps in the financing process.

Business finance is a field with a language of its own. Rather than interrupt the flow of our journey to define all of the finance terms used in this chapter, we have included definitions in a Glossary at the end of the book.

A few words of caution are in order. If you are raising money in any way other than approaching a bank for a loan, it is best to consult an attorney experienced in securities law before you approach investors. Most forms of raising money are subject to regulation under state and federal securities laws. Violating these laws may subject you to both civil and criminal penalties.

### *Multiple Sources*

❖ **Approach multiple sources of financing.**

❖ **Competition, or at least perceived competition, is the best way to close a deal on the most favorable terms.**

❖ **When presenting your concept to investors, realize that not only are you selling the investors on the idea of investing in your company but you are also training them to resell your concept to other investors that they may want to bring into the deal.**

❖ **Do not mass-mail your plan to multiple sources.**

The entrepreneur's goal should be to approach multiple sources of financing in several different investor categories, especially when looking for start-up financing. Then, as feedback is obtained, direction and efforts will become more focused and negotiations may be narrowed to a few of the most promising sources. There are at least three good reasons for using this approach:

First, it takes some trial and error to find out what type of investors will be most receptive to your concept. Obviously, as you were writing your business plan, you gained some insight in this area; but, there is nothing more reliable than going out and talking to prospects.

Second, it is important to have competition, or at least the perception of competition, to close a deal. If you are negotiating with multiple sources simultaneously, a sense of urgency is created which helps close the deal faster and possibly on more favorable terms.

Third, and most important, businesses are often funded by not just one investor, but groups of investors. Most investors do not like to invest alone. They want to have company – moral and financial support – especially when investing in start-ups. It is vital for the entrepreneur to realize this and try to help build investor alliances, while maintaining a sense of competition. This is one of the first opportunities for the entrepreneur to be creative and develop invaluable skills of negotiation. When selling your concept to raise capital, it is important to realize that not only are you selling the investors with your presentation but you are also training them to resell your concept to other investors that they may want to bring into the deal. Keeping this in mind should help you structure your business plan and presentation to convey a clear, concise, resaleable message.

Although we encourage approaching multiple sources, we also encourage selectivity in the sources you approach. Do not mass-mail your plan to multiple sources. Professional investors receive hundreds and thousands of business plans. Your plan may get very little, if any, attention if it is just mass-mailed. Contact financing sources by telephone or through a personal meeting or referral. Only send a business plan to those sources which show an interest in seeing it. In a cover letter attached to the plan, let the investors know that you will contact them within a week (or other specified time period) to set up a presentation and to answer questions concerning the plan. Then follow up.

### Presentation Hints

❖ One of the best shortcuts to obtaining financing is to be organized in your approach to investors.

❖ Keep your presentation as simple and to-the-point as possible – create excitement and avoid losing your listeners in too many numbers and too much detail.

❖ End your presentation with a summary of the key points that you want your listeners to remember.

❖ In following up with an investor, be persistent, but not a pest.

One of the best shortcuts to obtaining financing is to be organized in your approach to investors. Before approaching financing sources, have a plan for the type of deal that you want. Rather than approach prospective investors with some vague idea of what you want, in hopes of planning the deal together, have your own clear financing plan to sell to investors. Go in organized and in the driver's seat. You can always consider alternative proposals and be flexible in structuring a deal, but at least start out with a definite plan and with as much control of the situation as possible.

The worst thing you can do is go to a potential financing source and just say, "I am thinking about raising $10,000,000 for my business idea. What do you think I should do?" If you use this approach, you may as well scratch this source off the list of parties that will ever give you money.

Instead, be well-prepared with a good business plan and a good presentation. Developing a good business plan may take four to six weeks of full-time effort. Nevertheless, devoting the time to this step could substantially reduce the amount of time required to obtain financing once you start approaching financing sources.

When you present your business idea to investors, try to be creative and interesting in your approach. Keep your presentation as simple and to-the-point as possible – create excitement and avoid losing your listeners in too many numbers and too much detail. In our chapter on the business plan, we suggested that you include charts and as many graphics as possible to pictorially represent the numbers that you are projecting. In your presentation, you may want to use a flip chart with similar graphics that illustrate your projected growth in sales, revenues and profits. Show samples of your product. Tell your story with pictures and graphs, letting your investors review the detailed numbers and supporting schedules in your business plan later at their leisure. With your words, convey with enthusiasm the reasons why your company is going to succeed – the quality of your product, the uniqueness of your market niche, the experience and value of the people who are committed to your business. Use pictures and graphics to convey your message. As the cliché goes, "a picture is worth a thousand words." Your listeners will remember a graph picturing growing profits much better than they will remember a series of numbers.

End your presentation with a summary of the key points that you want your listeners to remember. You want to leave the investors with a clear concept of why your business is such an excellent investment opportunity. The people you are talking to will probably have to, in turn, sell the concept to others. Make it easy for them to remember the best selling points of your business.

In following up with an investor, be persistent, but not a pest. Ask when you should expect a response. Send a brief courtesy letter thanking the investors for their time and reiterating your key points. Also include any follow-up materials needed to answer open questions. If you do not receive a response within the expected time period, call and politely inquire about the status of review for your proposal.

### *Good Marketer*

❖ Either be a good marketer of your company or find a business partner or key staff person who can do so.

❖ A good marketer creates excitement so that people do not feel they are being asked for something but rather are being offered the privilege of participating in a wonderful opportunity.

❖ Market your business (without lying) so that you are not asking for money but, rather, you are giving the prospective investor the chance to participate in an exciting investment opportunity.

A real key to raising money is to be a good marketer. A good marketer creates excitement so that people do not feel they are being asked for something but rather are being offered the privilege of participating in a wonderful opportunity.

Suppose you are looking for $100,000 because you are going to make a widget. You could just go to investors and say, "I need $100,000 to produce a widget." You may be able to get your $100,000, but you won't get the best deal. Instead, go in to the investor and stress the strengths of your business or your idea. For example, show them that you are making the world's best widget; that you believe your customers will buy 100 million of them because of this or that factor; that you can manufacture them more cheaply than anyone else; that your sales staff is the best because you have taken the three best sales people in the industry; that you have the best mailing list, a clever marketing campaign, an exclusive international patent, etc.

All of this shows true business planning with logic and not just with numbers. It sells investors on why your business is poised for success. Investors will be excited by this type of approach. You are not asking them for something. You are giving them the privilege of making money off your hard work. Of course, the statements you make must be backed by fact and should be detailed in your business plan. Market your business (without lying) so that you are not asking for money but, rather, you are giving the prospective investor the chance to participate in an exciting investment opportunity.

If you do not have the confidence and drive to sell yourself and your concept to financing sources and customers, you will have an especially difficult time making it by yourself as an entrepreneur. That is not to say that there is no way for you to succeed. On the contrary, if you have a good business idea but you are not strong in marketing, instead of concentrating your efforts initially on selling the idea to financing sources, sell the idea to professional salespeople and marketers. Then, use them to help sell your concept to investors and to other key team members who have credibility in the industry.

To do this, you may have to give up significant pieces of ownership in the company to your business partners, but you will have a strong team that is more saleable to investors – 40% of something is better than 100% of nothing. Instead of starting off with a company valued from zero to $100,000, you may start off with a valuation of $1,000,000 or more simply because of the raw talent you have recruited. Potential investment sources will be impressed with the ability of you and your company to attract such talent.

## *Positive Attitude*

❖   With prospective investors, always remain confident and positive about yourself, your staff and the business. You are the backbone of the investment that they are considering.

❖   Once you have your strategy and approach organized, focus your attention on obtaining financing and try to complete the process as quickly as possible.

❖   Expect rejection initially, but learn from the rejection, and always ask for additional leads.

The importance of maintaining a positive attitude throughout the financing process cannot be stressed enough. With prospective investors, always remain confident and positive about yourself, your staff and the business. You are the backbone of the investment that they are considering.

You may ask, how am I supposed to be positive and confident when I have been repeatedly rejected by prospective investors after presenting to them the business concept into which I have poured my heart, soul, time and energies? Admittedly, staying positive under such circumstances may sometimes require a super-human effort.

Just remember that rejections are inevitable. It's just a matter of presenting your idea to enough sources until you find the "right" ones with whom to work. Screening your prospects via telephone conversations and researching other deals they have done will help minimize the number of "wasted" presentations. Also, maintaining the qualities that we discussed in the first chapter of this book, such as belief in yourself and your business idea, persistence, optimism, etc., will help support a positive attitude in the midst of rejections and set-backs.

No matter how well-prepared you are and how good your company is, there will be foolish investors who do not understand how brilliant you are or what a valuable investment opportunity you are presenting to them. You could talk to them until you were blue in the face and they still would not understand. When you realize that you are not getting anywhere with an investor that you are interested in and that you believe is right for you, step back. Think through the situation and realize that there are other ways to get investors excited besides talking to them until you are blue in the face. For example, you may be able to get what you want by creating a competitive feeling. Maybe you have also presented your ideas at another bank to Joe Blow, who always brings in all the good deals, and Joe Blow is bidding for your business. If the reluctant investor becomes aware of this, he may become more receptive. He does not want to be embarrassed when his boss finds out he missed another good deal that Joe Blow secured for his bank.

Although it is possible to turn a potential rejection into an approval for financing through your marketing techniques and through playing on the competitive instincts of investors, there will inevitably be situations in which you are rejected by financing sources that you approach. How do you stay "psyched up" during the financing process and cope with rejections?

The best way to stay psyched up is to start out with the right attitudes. Do not go in begging for money, but rather adopt the attitude that you are doing the investor a favor by providing this investment opportunity. Go in prepared and organized. Do not drag out the process. Once you have your strategy and approach organized, focus your attention on obtaining financing and try to complete the process as quickly as possible. One of the greatest demoralizing factors in looking for funds is to have time dragging on with nothing happening. If you are organized in your approach and you concentrate your efforts on securing the financing in a short period of time, it is easy to stay charged up and excited about the prospects of winning the financing you are seeking.

Expect rejection initially, but learn from the rejection. Find out why the investors said no – do they not have enough money; are they not interested in investing in businesses in your industry; or do they question the validity of your business concept?

Maybe you need to modify your approach or rethink your business plan. Make your first two or three calls on investors that are not your best prospects. Approach them as an experiment, recognizing that you may not get what you are after, but not being concerned with the rejection. Use these meetings as practice for your presentation and as an opportunity to receive feedback. Then, after these practice meetings, you should feel primed for the meetings with your best prospects, because you will be better prepared for what to expect.

Whenever prospects turn down the opportunity to invest in your business, do not become defensive, bitter or argumentative. Simply thank them for their time. Then, in addition to requesting an explanation of why they have turned you down, ask for leads or referrals to other financing sources that might be more receptive to investing in your business. Always keep the chain of referrals or leads going and do not burn bridges. Often, if one of the referrals says "yes" to investing in your business, the referring party re-examines the concept and participates in the deal, too.

### New v. Tried Concept

❖ **Recognize that financing a business based on a brand new concept is usually more difficult than financing a business in an existing but emerging industry.**

Before you attempt to finance your idea, recognize that the ease with which you find financing may depend on the type of business idea that you have. If your idea is for a product or business that is completely new and different, finding money in the initial financing stages may be more difficult than it would if the idea were a variation of an existing product or service in an emerging industry.

Initially funding brand new concepts is often difficult because there is generally more risk involved with brand new ideas. You do not know what sort of market there will be for the product or service offered by the business, so you have no actual basis for your projections. The first person to try to raise money for an idea is probably going to have a much harder time raising the money than will the second, third and fourth persons who try to fund the same idea. On the other hand, if you are the seventh, eighth, ninth or tenth person to try to develop the idea, you may not be able to find the funding because you are too late. The timing of your efforts to fund a particular idea may be critical in determining whether or not you will secure the financing you are seeking.

### *Amount and Type of Financing*

❖   It is often easier to raise large sums of money than it is to raise small sums.

❖   Try to raise a little more in equity and arrange to borrow a lot more than you think you will need.

Contrary to what many people may think, it may be more difficult for you to raise a small amount of money (less than $500,000) for your business than it is to raise a large amount ($1,000,000 or more). Because of the time and energy required to evaluate investment opportunities, professional investors would prefer to invest larger chunks of money in a few good business opportunities rather than investing lots of little chunks of money in so many businesses that it is impractical to keep an eye on such investments. So, for example, it may be easier to raise $1,000,000 by selling 10 people a $100,000 interest each, than it is to raise $100,000 by selling 20 people a $5,000 interest each.

If you only need a small sum now, but know that you will need a substantial amount more within the next year or two, you may have more success finding investors if you structure a financing proposal that seeks both amounts, but in stages. An investor may commit to a maximum sum of money to carry you through more than one phase of financing, with the right to draw against that amount as certain milestones are met.

For instance, if you know that you only need $50,000 now, but you believe you may need an additional $250,000 over the next six months and $700,000 over the following year, consider one investment proposal for raising $1,000,000, rather than separate proposals for $50,000, $250,000 and $700,000. You might reach an agreement with the investors to provide $50,000 now, with a commitment to provide the remainder of the money as specific projects are completed, a certain volume of orders are received, a particular licensing agreement is executed, or certain contracts are awarded.

There are two basic forms of financing for a company – debt and equity financing. Debt financing is money that is borrowed. At some point it must be repaid. Equity financing is money that someone invests in a business in exchange for an ownership interest in the business. The major advantage of debt financing is that it does not require you to give up part of your ownership; the major disadvantage is that you are obligated to repay the money. Equity financing, on the other hand, does not have to be repaid, but requires you to give up part of your owner-ship in exchange for financing.

There are many different types of both debt fi-nancing (secured loans, unsecured loans and bonds, for example) and equity financing (common stock, preferred stock, warrants and limited partnership in-terests, to name a few). (See the definitions of these terms in the Glossary.) There are even some financ-ing arrangements that start out as debt, with a right to convert to equity at some later point, or vice versa. The various options and combinations are too exten-sive to describe in a book of this scope. If you are not experienced in business finance, you would be well-advised to read some business finance books or arti-cles and hire professional advisors. Become better ac-quainted with your options before completing your financing plan or approaching investors. Theoreti-cally, professionals should more than offset their cost by obtaining a higher valuation for your business.

Businesses are usually financed through a com-bination of debt and equity financing. The concept of raising a portion of the financing through selling equity and a portion through a loan or some other form of debt is called "leveraging" or "using lever-age." Using leverage makes sense for the entrepre-neur because it allows him or her to raise at least a portion of money for the business without giving up ownership.

The amount of debt in relation to the amount of equity for a business is referred to as the "debt-to-equity ratio." A business with $100,000 of equity (assets minus liabilities) that has $200,000 of loans outstanding has a debt-to-equity ratio of 2 to 1 ($200,000 divided by $100,000). "Acceptable" levels of debt-to-equity could range from a low of 2 to 1 to a high of 10 to 1 or even higher, depending upon a variety of factors, including the state of the industry, economic climate, and performance history and/or prospects of the company, to name a few.

Some of the primary factors to consider in evaluating different financing options are: (1) If you are selling equity, will you retain enough of an ownership interest to maintain control of the company now and through future rounds of financing? (2) If you are assuming debt, will you be able to meet debt repayment obligations, according to your cash-flow projections? (3) What are the tax consequences of the financing package? and (4) Will the investment package and investor that you are considering leave room for you to bring in additional financing or investors in the future?

Use your business plan and budget to help determine the amounts of financing you think you will need and the timing of that financing. Never underestimate the amount of money you need. On the other hand, do not raise too much money by selling equity too soon because you will unnecessarily dilute your interest in the company. Always try to raise a little more in equity than you think you need and arrange to borrow a lot more than you think you will need. We don't mean that you should actually borrow more than you need, saddling yourself with a lot of debt you can't repay. We just mean that you should arrange for lines of credit or other debt in amounts that are greater than what you might think you would need so that you can draw on these funds, if and when needed. That way, you will have the ability to quickly respond to financial opportunities and to weather cash-flow fluctuations without a crisis.

## Selection Criteria

❖ Select investors based not only upon financial considerations but also upon whether or not you will feel comfortable working with them.

❖ It is better to be a small investment for a large investor than to be a large investment for a small investor.

When selecting potential sources of financing, you are, in a sense, selecting a business partner. Therefore, your goal should not only be to get the best deal possible but also to select sources with which you believe your company will have a comfortable working relationship. Sometimes a particular bank, investor, or other financing source will be one that you will continue to work with throughout the life of your company. Other times, you may find that you will work with a particular financing source for a period of time. Then, later, you may discover that your company has outgrown the ability of the source to provide further financial support or that the relationship between the source and your company is no longer working smoothly. You should approach a relationship with a financing source with the attitude that you are looking for a long-term business relationship. You should also realize, however, that your needs may change. You should, therefore, be prepared to develop other financial relationships in the future, as necessary for the growth and success of your business.

You should look for sources that are reasonable, level-headed, understand your business, are willing to stand behind you, and are not straining their investment limits to invest in your company. If you go with a source that would be pushing its investment limits to invest in your company, you will not have any leeway to use that source to finance further growth. Furthermore, such a source might place excessive restrictions on your business in an attempt to protect its "large" investment. It is better to be a small investment for a large investor than to be a large investment for a small investor.

## *Ongoing Relations With Your Investors*

❖ **Do not promise more to your investors than you can deliver.**

As we pointed out in the previous section, you should expect most of your relationships with investors to be long-term. You may want to call on these investors for business advice or for additional financing. Therefore, you should relate to these investors in ways that will promote a positive working relationship.

Of course, if you are dealing with a lender, the best way to maintain a smooth relationship is to make your payments on time and to build a good credit history. If you are dealing with equity investors, you should work out some sort of periodic system to report financial information and progress.

Whatever you do, do not promise more than you can deliver. You must build credibility with your financial sources. Do not promise monthly financial reports if you do not have the resources to deliver reports on a monthly basis. Arrange to deliver financial reports on a quarterly basis instead. It is better to be realistic about what you can reasonably deliver and then stick by your word than to promise more than you can deliver and then constantly go back on your word. If you do not deliver what you have promised, you will have nervous investors, and nervous investors may then try to come in and run your business to protect their investment.

## *Financing Phases*

❖ **Financing a business is usually not a one-time occurrence.**

❖ **The financing phases required for a specific business vary depending upon the type of business.**

Financing a business is usually not a one-time occurrence, particularly for a growth-oriented business. It is an ongoing process. As a business grows, additional funds are needed to meet increased demand, expand into new markets, acquire additional assets or inventory, hire additional staff, etc. Different amounts, types and sources of financing are needed at different stages of growth.

Typically, a successful entrepreneurial venture will raise capital in phases that have been loosely labelled seed capital, start-up, second round, mezzanine and initial public offering (which are defined in the Glossary). There are many variations of these phases, but a general understanding of the purpose, timing and potential sources for each of these phases, as summarized in the chart on the following page, is helpful. The next subsection of this chapter provides more detail concerning various financing sources.

The financing phases required for a specific business vary depending upon the type of business. Some businesses (such as manufacturing companies) may go through all of the financing phases listed in the preceding paragraph, sometimes more than once, while others (such as a small retail or service business) may require only one or two stages of financing.

## Financing Phases and Sources

| Financing Phase | Purpose | Sources* | Comments |
|---|---|---|---|
| Seed Capital | Develop Prototype | 1,2,3,6, 8, 9, 11 | Equity only |
| Start-up | Set Up Production | 1,2,3,6, 7,8,9,11 | Equity only |
| Second Round | Begin full-scale operations, marketing, selling | 4,5,6,7, 8,10 | Usually, equity in conjunction with debt financing from a bank or factor |
| Mezzanine | Increase market penetration and working capital | 4,5,6,7, 10,12 | Usually, both debt and equity financing |
| Initial Public Offering | Liquidity for founders, investors, and employees; fund new products, expansion and acquisitions | 4,7,12 | Opportunity for entrepreneur and early-stage investors to convert some stock to cash |

\* The following are codes for sources: 1=personal funds; 2=family and friends; 3=private investors; 4=banks; 5=factoring; 6=venture capitalists; 7=investment bankers; 8=corporate sponsors; 9=state and federal government sources; 10=customer financing; 11=grants; 12=foreign resources.

There is no hard and fast rule for the period of time each phase of financing should last. Raising money is such a time-consuming proposition that financing sources usually like to see a round of financing cover at least a year's financing needs. Sometimes the time period may be shorter, however, because of the nature of the product. For example, if you are developing a prototype product, you may raise seed capital to develop that prototype over a six-month period. Then at the end of that period, after the prototype has been tested, new financing will be needed to produce and market the product. As pointed out earlier, however, a financing commitment may be negotiated to cover more than one phase.

## *Financing Sources*

❖ **A key to effectively financing your company is to know which types of sources to approach at which phase of your business development. It is also important to know how to relate to each source.**

❖ **Investors in your company, unless they are family and friends, are investing for <u>one</u> reason – they want to make money.**

There are a variety of potential sources of debt and equity financing for your business. A key to effectively financing your company is to know which types of sources to approach at which phase of your business development (See the chart in the preceding section, "Financing Phases."). It is also important to know how to relate to each source. Each financing source has an important role to play, but it is crucial for you to know how best to use each source so that you gain the maximum benefit without giving up too much of your company.

When dealing with investors, remember that investors in your company, unless they are family and friends, are investing for one reason – they want to make money. You want to trust them and use them, but with caution and, perhaps, with expert advice.

How do you find which investors to approach? You do a lot of homework collecting names. Then you find out as much as you can about each prospect so that you concentrate your efforts on the ones that may have an interest in the type of deal that you are proposing.

There are countless ways to find out the identity of prospective investors. Ask your attorney, accountant and business contacts for references; go to the library or book store for reference books; look through magazines such as *Inc.*; contact your state government and local universities; approach trade associations for your industry. Many communities and universities have active venture capital clubs and/or incubators for entrepreneurial ventures that are excellent sources of contacts and information.

The remainder of this section discusses some of the major sources of financing for businesses.

### *Personal Funds*

Generally, entrepreneurs must invest some personal funds in their businesses before others will invest. Most investors want to see that the entrepreneur is committed enough to the business to put some personal assets at risk. The amount of investment from the entrepreneur that other investors expect to see will vary depending on such factors as the complexity of the business, the prior business success track record of the entrepreneur, the uniqueness of the product or service, and whether or not the business is part of an industry that is considered to be an attractive investment area.

The aspiring entrepreneur often has little or no money to invest personally. In this situation prospective investors may look for the amount of "sweat equity" (hours without pay) that the founder has devoted to starting the business. They may also place limitations on compensation and/or require that the founder pledge assets, such as a house or insurance policy, as security.

### *Family and Friends*

One of the most common ways of financing, particularly for small businesses, is to obtain debt or equity financing from family and friends. There is nothing wrong with using this source of financing. The more speculative the business, however, the more careful you should be about accepting money from family and friends and the more you should consider approaching professional investors.

If your business turns out to be a success and you did not go to your family and friends first to offer them equity in the business, they may be angry with you. On the other hand, if you go to family and friends too early and your business turns out to be unsuccessful, you may lose their money. Then they may be even more angry.

Once you are fairly certain that you have a business that will succeed, then you can think about offering family and friends an equity interest. Bring them in early, but not necessarily during the seed-capital phase of your financing unless they are wealthy or will only be contributing a small amount and will not miss the money if you lose it. Do not take someone's life savings to fund your seed-capital phase. It is not worth the risk. Remember, if you are successful, you can always give family and friends gifts, money or an interest in your business without putting them at risk. Use family and friends for moral support, a role that they cannot fulfill if they are too heavily invested in your venture.

## *Private Investors*

Recent studies have shown that entrepreneurial ventures are funded more by private investors than by any other source. These studies estimate that over 700,000 private investors annually invest in almost 100,000 different businesses.

Private investors are typically successful business people who like to invest in new companies within their industries or related industries. Some are willing to explore new industries, depending upon the venture and its prospects as presented by the entrepreneur. Most, however, prefer to invest within an industry that they know well. Private investors can often help the entrepreneur not only by providing financing, but also by providing advice, contacts and introductions in their industry.

Private investors are generally greater risk-takers than venture capitalists or other early-round sources and are willing to accept lower rates of return on their investments. For example, a typical private investor might want to see a 20% return on investment, while a venture capitalist might expect at least 30%.

Private investors will usually ask questions similar to those listed in the "Venture Capitalists" section of this chapter. However, they are often less rigid in their expectations because of their knowledge of the industry and their belief that they can help the business succeed.

## *Banks*

Although we talk about "banks" in this section, most of our comments would also apply to the broader range of commercial lenders, including such sources as savings and loan institutions, insurance companies and pension funds.

Banks want to lend money because that is the way that they make money – from interest on their loans. They want to receive those interest payments, so for as long as you are a safe credit risk (have the ability to repay the loan) and you do not ever miss a payment, the bank may not care if the principal ever gets repaid.

What do banks look for when evaluating a loan request? The bank looks at: whether or not the business will generate enough income and cash flow to meet the interest obligations on the loan; whether or not the borrower has a history of meeting credit obligations; and the borrower's ability to repay from personal assets should the business fail.

Banks usually ask prospective borrowers several standard questions: (1) Do you have three years' tax returns for yourself and your business? This is always an obstacle for the new business and leads the conversation to an early end or towards talk of personal guarantees and security interests. (2) Do you have financial statements? Ideally you will have financial statements that show a currently profitable business. It is not unusual, however, to see a company with losses and a negative net worth during the start-up period. If the net worth is negative, it will probably be necessary to have additional equity ready to fund the business in conjunction with the loan. Most lenders will not make loans to companies with a negative net worth. (3) Do you have a business plan with financial projections? The bank wants to see that the entrepreneur has a well-thought-out plan and that the business has sufficient growth potential to entice the bank to want to begin relations now in hopes of eventually gaining a large client.

Simultaneously negotiate with the banks for a loan when negotiating with other investors for equity financing. Working with both the banks and the equity investors simultaneously will help determine the most favorable balance of debt and equity financing for your company at a particular point in time. The relative amounts of debt and equity financing that are best for a company and acceptable to a lender will depend upon such factors as the ability of the company to comfortably meet its loan payment obligations (as well as other liabilities) out of cash flow, the valuation placed on the business, and the aggressiveness of the banks at the time financing is sought.

Typically, a bank would prefer to see a 2 to 1 debt-to-equity ratio or better. This means that the total current liabilities (accounts payable, taxes payable, salaries earned but not paid, and bank debt) are not more than two times the equity (retained earnings plus capital). Different banks at different times will lend at higher debt-to-equity ratios. It is not unusual for a bank to accept a debt-to-equity ratio of up to 4 or 5 to 1. In competitive markets for "hot" industries, a bank may go as high as 10 to 1 or more. It pays to shop around. Shopping around for lenders may pay off not only with respect to the amount of financing you are able to secure, but also with respect to other negotiated items, such as interest rate, length of term, commitment and origination fees, security and guarantees.

Consider establishing working relationships with more than one bank to broaden your options and to keep a little competition going. Then, if one of your banks starts getting nervous because your debt load is somewhat high in relation to equity, that bank may still be willing to work with you. To them, the only thing worse than their nervousness over your debt load is their fear that you will take your business to another bank.

What type of loan should you try to obtain? The various lending institutions will market a myriad of loans under a variety of clever titles and descriptions. For example, common categories of loans include asset-based, short-term working capital, term, line of credit, factoring, accounts receivable or inventory financing, equity-based, secured, unsecured, and various combinations thereof.

Despite all the fancy names, just remember that the concept of lending is pretty simple – the lender wants timely interest payments and sufficient security to know that, even if the business fails or the lender forces liquidation, there are adequate assets to repay the bank in full.

The lender typically wants current asset security for its loan. The most common arrangement is to (1) loan against a percentage of accounts receivable and/or inventory, (2) obtain a security interest in all the assets of the company and (3) require personal guarantees from the owners. Typically, a bank might start with a loan equal to 70-80% of eligible receivables that are less than ninety days outstanding. Then, as confidence is gained, the lender might raise the loan or line of credit to 80-90% of receivables under 90 days old, plus a percentage of inventory, perhaps 25% initially, increasing later to 50%. In addition, the bank might place a dollar limit on the loan amount so that the debt-to-equity ratio will remain under a certain level. The maximum loan amount might increase as equity increases.

Let the bank be half traditional bank and half venture capitalist by lending money more aggressively than banks usually prefer. Of course, the location of a bank – the general economic conditions in the area and the degree of competition among banks – will influence the aggressiveness of the loan department.

Some of the more aggressive banks have investment divisions. Such banks may make loans to you on the condition that they will also get warrants or options for an equity position in your company or that their investment division gets first rights for equity financing. These banks are serving not only as lenders, but also as venture capitalists or investment bankers. Usually such banks are less greedy than venture capitalists in demanding equity because they are already making money from the interest on the loans they have made to you. The venture capitalist, on the other hand, is giving you money for an ownership interest in your company with little or no present return on that money. The venture capitalist will realize a return only after your company has grown to the point where the equity owned by the venture capitalist may be sold for a healthy profit through a public offering or to some other investor.

## *Factoring*

In some industries, most notably the garment industry, it is common for companies to factor their accounts receivable rather than use accounts receivable financing from banks. Factoring basically involves a company's selling or transferring its accounts receivable to a factor. By acquiring the accounts receivable, the factor assumes the risk of default if the receivables cannot be collected. The factor and the company negotiate a fee for this service. The fee can be paid through discounting the receivables or paying a commission. Factoring generally costs more than bank financing but can work out to be less expensive after calculating the potential cost of bad debts and the expense of maintaining a collections department.

## *Venture Capitalists*

Venture capitalists acquire ownership interests in privately-held companies that they believe will grow substantially and pay a healthy return within a reasonable period of time (usually three to five years). They risk investing in a start-up or growing company in hopes of realizing a much higher return than they would receive through more traditional, "safer" investments.

The return expected by a venture capitalist may come in the form of dividends but more often comes from selling the venture capitalist's equity after it has appreciated to an expected level due to the company's growth. The equity may be sold to public investors through a public offering, to other private investors or, perhaps, to the entrepreneur.

Venture capitalists come in all shapes and sizes. Some are venture capital companies funded by private and/or public sources. Others are subsidiaries of financial institutions (such as insurance companies or pension funds) that diversify their investments.

Venture capitalists have specific types of deals that they want to invest in. Only a few invest in start-up companies, while many more invest in later-stage financing. Sometimes the venture capitalist will invest only in specific types of industries – high technology, manufacturing, etc. Venture capitalists will usually quote a range of amounts that they will invest, for example, no less than $500,000 and no more than $2,000,000. They have specific goals for the amount of money they want to make over a period of time with each investment – for instance, perhaps they want to make 3 to 5 times their initial investment over a period of three years. You need to know the specific goals of each venture capitalist that you approach so that you will know how best to negotiate with each.

The best way to know whether or not to contact a particular venture capitalist about financing your business is to contact the company on the telephone. Ask a few key questions regarding the size of investments the company makes and whether or not the company invests in businesses similar to yours. You may not want to approach a venture capitalist that has heavily invested in a direct competitor of your business. However, you want the venture capitalists to have some understanding of your industry so that you do not have to educate them about your industry from scratch.

Most venture capitalists look very closely at the track record of the founders of the company. A large part of their investment is an investment in people.

They want to be sure that the people running the company are going to be able to build the company successfully enough to give them the payback they are looking for within the projected time period.

Venture capitalists often have the reputation of being greedy and requesting too much ownership and control for the amount of money they anticipate investing. There is a certain amount of truth associated with the reputation. However, there have also been many examples of venture capitalists placing a surprisingly high value on a business in which they are investing.

The best assurance of structuring a favorable deal with venture capitalists is to be prepared. "Prepared" means having a well-conceived business plan, a solid understanding of your product and market, and your key personnel identified and on board.

Venture capitalists will typically ask such questions as: 1) Does the product work? 2) Who is the target market and how do you know they need the product? 3) How do you plan to get the product into the customer's hands? 4) Who is your competition and why will you be more successful than they? 5) What market share do you expect and how large is the total market? 6) What kind of expertise do you and your key employees have in this field? 7) How much will it cost to get the product to market? to support it? to obtain raw materials? to advertise? to set up data-processing systems? to meet other expenses of doing business?

The goal of your presentation to venture capitalists is to excite their interest in the product idea and convince them that you are the right person to invest in. If possible, answer potential questions before they are asked. Questions may imply doubt in your abilities or the business concept and may put you in a defensive position. It is better to anticipate the potential doubts and questions and provide persuasive assurances and answers before the questions can even be verbalized. Practicing a presentation and role-playing are effective methods for developing confidence and anticipating questions. If you play the role of venture capitalist evaluating someone else's business plan or your own, you may gain surprising insights into how you should approach presenting your plan.

## *Investment Bankers*

Investment bankers can be good sources for structuring deals to raise money, such as private placements or public offerings, and for assisting you with finding candidates to acquire your company, should you decide to sell. The key to working with investment bankers is finding the ones that are right for you. They come in all shapes and sizes. You should find one that is familiar with your industry and that is accustomed to working on deals of the size and type that you are proposing. There are books published on an annual basis that list all of the investment bankers by the types of businesses that they specialize in and the types and numbers of deals they have done. (See "Financial Information" in Appendix C.) Perhaps the best way to find the most appropriate investment bankers to approach is to talk to people who have dealings with the investment banking industry, such as accountants, attorneys, commercial bankers, business school faculty and financial officers of other non-competing companies.

Investment bankers may work with you on a contingency basis, requiring payment only for money that is actually raised, or they may require a combination of fees for services plus a contingent fee based on money raised. The smaller the deal or the smaller the company, the more likely the investment banker will require some sort of retainer-fee arrangement to ensure they will be compensated for the time expended. From your standpoint, of course, you want to arrange a deal where the investment banker gets paid only if money is raised, except, perhaps, for approved out-of-pocket expenses. If you are paying a monthly retainer, the investment banker representative you are dealing with will have less incentive to find the money or close the deal – he or she may get too comfortable collecting those monthly payments without having to produce the financing you are seeking.

You want to structure a deal that will motivate people to close a deal as quickly as possible at the highest possible value for your company. One way to give investment bankers an incentive to arrive at the highest possible valuation for your company is to compensate them at a higher percentage for a higher value being placed on your company. Traditionally, sliding-scale commissions have been structured to give a lower percentage as more money is raised. For example, a typical formula is 5% of the first million dollars raised, 4% of the second million, 3% of the third million, 2% of the fourth million and 1% of the fifth million and above. By increasing the percentage instead of decreasing it, you will give an added incentive to raise more money.

### *Public Offering*

Conducting a public offering is one method of obtaining later-stage financing – an incredibly complex, time-consuming and expensive method that would require volumes to describe in any depth. We list it because it is an alternative to consider, but we will comment on this option only briefly.

A company's founders may dream of the day when they will take the company public. Going public: (1) allows the founders and their original investors to realize a return on their investment by selling some or all of their stock through the public market; (2) generates a certain image boost, since many people equate a public company with success or stability; (3) provides a carrot to entice additional key employees who are interested in owning a liquid equity position in the company they work for; (4) supplies an injection of cash for expansion; and (5) gives access to the public market for future capital needs.

On the other hand, a public offering has certain down sides. Once a company goes public, it will be just that – "public." Detailed records concerning the finances and operations of the company will become a matter of public record and must be updated regularly. Anyone wanting to know about the company, including competitors and customers, as well as stockholders, will have access to these records. The founders, officers and directors of the company will be accountable to a large number of stockholders and will constantly be held answerable for actions that negatively affect the value of the stock. Conducting a public offering and meeting filing requirements is very expensive and time consuming.

A successful public offering requires a number of professionals, particularly lawyers, auditors and investment bankers, plus a professional management team, including an in-house chief financial officer. If you decide that the advantages of a public offering outweigh its disadvantages for your company, these people will guide you through this complicated process. However, a few words of wisdom are in order – read at least one book on the subject and delegate responsibilities, but stay closely involved in the process – there is a lot at stake.

## *Franchising*

If your business idea involves a product or service that you want to market through multiple locations, one option for financing your venture may be to franchise the concept rather than to try to come up with enough money to open multiple locations yourself. Suppose it costs $200,000 to open each of your locations and you want to open 100 locations. Instead of coming up with $20,000,000 to open all of the locations yourself, you may instead be able to raise $500,000 to $1,000,000 to develop and market the franchise and then sell franchises to other people to open the additional locations.

When you sell a franchise, you sell to others the licensed right to open and operate businesses bearing your franchised name. You will provide guidance to the franchisee for opening and operating the business and will grant a license to use the trademarks and logos of the franchise system. Each purchaser of a franchise (the "franchisee") will: (1) put up the money to develop the franchised location, (2) own and operate the franchise, (3) pay you an up-front fee for your assistance in getting the business started, (4) pay you an ongoing royalty for the continuing right to participate in the franchise system and (5) in many instances, pay a fee for centralized advertising of the franchise system. For franchising to work, you must have a marketable name and a concept that can be duplicated fairly easily from one location to another. You must also have the ability to control the quality of

products or services offered at the franchised locations. Furthermore, the concept must generate
enough profits at the franchisee level to pay the franchisor an ongoing royalty, while still leaving the
franchisee an attractive profit margin.

## Corporate Sponsors

When looking for a way to finance your business, think creatively. Perhaps your best source of financing is not a traditional financing source such as a
bank or a venture capitalist. Maybe  the best source of
financing for your business idea is a corporation that
somehow stands to gain if your business succeeds.
People who have decided to be intrapreneurs rather
than entrepreneurs are, in effect, finding corporate
sponsors to finance their ideas. Corporate sponsors
may be excellent investors for the entrepreneur, as
well.

For example, perhaps you are currently an employee of a manufacturing business and you have
spotted a marketplace where the products your company manufactures are not being effectively marketed. You may be able to structure a new business
reselling the products of the manufacturing company
into this new marketplace and you may be able to receive financial backing from the manufacturing
company to do it. Such financial backing could be an
up-front cash advance to get started, lenient terms for
paying for the inventory, or shared office space
and/or office staff. Receiving a credit line or lengthy
periods for payment for inventory from the manufacturer can solve one of the biggest financial burdens
faced by new companies. You can start your business
with a good stock of inventory but not have to pay
for that inventory until you have had a reasonable

time to resell it and collect the cash from the customer.

The prior example is just one idea for receiving financial backing from a corporation. Think about the types of companies that would benefit if your business succeeds. Then try to think of ways to receive financial backing from such companies. If you can think of a corporation that would benefit significantly from the success of your business, that corporation may advance the money you need in the form of a loan or equity. The corporation may be motivated more by what your proposed business could do to increase the market for its products than by the potential return on its investment in your business. Therefore, you may be able to structure a much more favorable deal with the corporation than you could with a bank or venture capitalist.

If you decide to approach corporate sponsors, carefully consider how to protect your idea in the event the corporation wishes to implement your idea without your assistance. Ideas, in and of themselves, are not protectable through avenues such as patents, copyrights or trademarks. Some ways to protect your idea would include requesting that the corporation execute a tightly-drafted non-disclosure agreement before you present the idea. You should also try to somehow make yourself an indispensable part of the concept (perhaps because you own the patent or have the trade secret that will make the idea workable, or have progressed so far with the development of the idea that to duplicate it would require substantial time and energy).

## State and Federal Government Sources

There are a surprising number of government sources of financing. Many states have economic development divisions that engage in venture capital financing and/or provide debt financing through loans or loan guarantees. Sometimes this financing is funded through the sale of industrial revenue bonds. There are also a variety of financing opportunities through federal sources. If you are interested in exploring sources of government financing, a starting point is to contact your state's economic development office and the Small Business Administration.

## Customer Financing

Sometimes you can finance the production of products by taking advance orders from customers and having them prepay. You may be able to develop a prototype of the product; take orders based on the prototype; require pre-payment, or at least partial pre-payment, for the products ordered; then use the money to pay for the production of the product.

Mail-order and periodical publications sold by subscription (magazines and newsletters) are two industries where customers pay for products significantly in advance of the delivery of those products. In the mail-order business, for example, an ad is run or a catalogue picturing the product is distributed. The customer orders the product, often sending a check or using a credit card at the time the order is placed, but not expecting delivery for a specified period of time. The owner of the company is then able to use the pre-payments to finance the production of the product. A word of caution is in order, however. Federal Trade Commission regulations require delivery of mail-order products within thirty days from the date the order is received, unless a longer time is specified in the mail-order advertising. Furthermore, if a shipment is not going to be made on time, the purchaser must be given notice of the delay and a right to cancel the order. Operators of mail-order businesses must comply with these and other applicable federal and state requirements.

Another method of customer financing is to get your customers to actually invest in your business. For example, if you are a supplier to a large corporation, that corporation might be interested in investing in your business to enable you to expand more rapidly to meet the corporation's increased demand. The support of such a company may, in turn, lend credibility to your business that will help in securing loans and raising additional money from other sources.

### Grants

Certain industries – particularly in the medical, health and safety fields – are often funded with grants from universities, business, trusts or the government. Obtaining a grant is a process similar to raising money from banks or venture capitalists, as far as documenting and selling your concept. It is just a different set of people and paperwork. Information on grants may be obtained from a variety of resources, including but not limited to universities, consultants, banks, trade associations and some government offices.

## Foreign Resources

Sometimes it is possible to find foreign investors to finance a business or product idea. Some of these investors are cash-rich individuals or groups looking strictly for profitable returns on their investments. Others might be companies interested in financing a business idea because of some potential benefit in addition to receiving dividends or interest.

For example, if your idea is to manufacture and distribute a product, you may be able to find financing for your operations through foreign manufacturers. A foreign manufacturer eager to penetrate the lucrative United States market may be willing to assume the risk of manufacturing your new product either for an equity stake in your business, a percentage of future revenues, or both. A further benefit of exploring relationships with foreign manufacturers is not only the potential for financing, but also the fact that manufacturing costs are often lower abroad than in the United States.

There are a number of consultants and brokers who help locate foreign financing sources, or you can simply work through embassy contacts here or abroad for leads on investors and companies to approach. Some embassies may even assist with arranging meetings.

Of course, obtaining financing from foreign sources adds some additional risks – differences in laws and customs, possible changes in exchange rates, import/export regulations, and potential shipment complications, to name a few. These risks should be realistically evaluated when deciding whether or not to go this route.

## *Additional Financing Alternatives* *for Ongoing Businesses*

Suppose you are an operational company that has received prior rounds of financing. Now you need some bridge financing to meet your financial obligations, but your existing investors are unwilling to provide additional money. One way to see your company through cash-flow crunches is to reduce cash drains by selling off non-productive assets or divisions of your company. Another alternative is to acquire another business that may be generating cash flow and use the cash flow from the second business to finance the first business. It may be easier to raise money for such an acquisition than it is to raise money for bridge financing. Still another option for generating additional funds is to set up a research and development division that can receive financing from a grant or through other financing sources. Then arrange for your primary company to receive a management fee for managing that research and development division. Working out extended credit terms with suppliers is still another way to ease a cash-flow crunch. As with many other aspects of running a business, a key to solving cash-flow problems is to be creative and flexible.

## *Structuring The Deal*

❖ If possible, tie your financial agreements with investors to the potential growth of your business.

How do you know how much equity to give up to investors? That is one of the world's most difficult financial questions. The question is particularly difficult when you are trying to raise money for a start-up operation because there is so little information available on which to base the value of the stock of the company. The lower the value placed on the stock, the greater the percentage of stock an investor will receive, and the less the entrepreneur will keep.

In the eyes of the entrepreneur, the venture capitalists usually want too much equity. This situation is often overcome in one of several ways. First, the entrepreneur might agree to the venture capitalist's absurdly low valuation of the stock on the condition that, if certain milestones or sales levels are met on time, the next level of financing will be at a much higher valuation. Then the average of the two rounds of financing balance out to both parties' mutual satisfaction. Another option is to agree on a sliding scale valuation, in which the starting point of the scale is the venture capitalist's valuation. However, if certain milestones or sales and profit levels are met on time, then the valuation automatically adjusts over a six-month to three-year period. Further examples of dealing with the dilemma of valuing start-ups are given later in this section.

No matter whether the company is a start-up or an established business, an investor expects to receive an equity interest in a company that is based on the relationship between the money provided by that investor and the value of the company. The tricky part of the equation is that equity investors use all sorts of formulas and techniques to place a value on a company. Investors usually value the company using several of these formulas and then concentrate on the ones that will give them the greatest equity interest.

Most often, a **multiple of earnings** (also referred to as a **price/earnings (P/E) ratio**) is used to value a business. As the name implies, this method places a value on the company by multiplying the company's annual earnings by a selected number. Typically, investors will look at forecasted earnings twelve months into the future, as presented in the business plan. Then, based upon such projections, as well as the previous financial history (if any), the overall appeal of the business and entrepreneur, the current attractiveness of the particular industry, and the current status of the stock market, the investors will select a multiple of earnings as the basis for valuing a company. Multiples can vary dramatically based on the variables listed above – easily ranging from 3 to 25 times earnings, depending upon the current status of any of the variables. Timing is very important.

To illustrate the application of the multiple-of-earnings concept, if you have forecast $500,000 of after-tax earnings for twelve months into the future and the investors have calculated the value of your company using a price/earnings multiple of 10, the valuation prior to capitalization would be $5,000,000 ($500,000 X 10). Assuming you raised $1,000,000, you would give up 20% ($1,000,000 ÷ $5,000,000) of the company and have an after-capitalization value of $6,000,000 ($5,000,000 plus the $1,000,000 of new capital). Always clarify with investors whether their valuation is based on the value before or after capitalization.

Another formula for valuing your company is to say that is is worth "x" times the book value. This method is rarely used with start-up companies because little or no equity exists.

When calculating the percentage of equity interest expected in return for an investment, investors look not only at formulas such as the ones described above. They also look at other transactions that have occurred in your industry and your strength in the marketplace. Industry comparisons may not be as simple as they may seem at first blush. The investors' classification of your industry could have a tremendous impact on the valuation that is given to your company, so you should be sure that your business is being properly categorized. For example, suppose your company distributes computer products to the government. Your company may be valued much more highly if you are categorized as a government contractor rather than as a reseller of computer products. This may occur because the latter category may be saturated with companies, while the category of government contractor may be an emerging growth field for companies distributing computer products and your company may be the market leader in that area.

There are a wide variety of ways that you may structure your agreements with investors. We recommend that you try to tie your financial agreements with investors to the potential growth of your company. For instance, if you are a start-up business with no sales or if you are trying to sell your business and are having difficulty reaching an agreement with the investor as to the value of the company, you can use what is called an "earn-out" or a "sliding-scale valuation."

The following examples explain how these types of deals work. They are described in very simple terms to illustrate the concepts. To actually structure a deal employing any of these concepts requires extreme care and the advice of professionals with expertise in such matters. The tax, control, securities and other legal and financial aspects of such deals are complex and must be carefully evaluated and structured.

Assume you are a start-up business and you claim your business is worth $10,000,000 based on your projections of $1,000,000 in earnings and a price/earnings multiple of 10. Assume also that your investors say your business is worth only $5,000,000. They agree that a price/earnings multiple of 10 is appropriate, but they think you may only show earnings of $500,000. What you can do is structure an earn-out agreement. You agree with the investors that the business is worth only $5,000,000, and that they will give you $1,000,000 in exchange for 20% of the stock of the company. But you also agree that if you meet certain milestones, their ownership percentage diminishes. For example, you could agree that you could earn back up to 10% of the stock you have sold them by achieving earnings in excess of $500,000 over the next year. You could agree that for every $50,000 over $500,000 in earnings, you will earn back 1% of the stock you sold them. That way, if you meet your earnings projections of $1,000,000 (which would mean the company was valued at $10,000,000 instead of $5,000,000) you will then own 90% of the company and they will own 10% for their $1,000,000 investment. If you succeed, both parties should be satisfied. Even though the investors' ownership percentage has been reduced, the formula agreed to by both parties was not altered. Both parties agreed that a multiple of 10 on the next year's earnings was an agreeable formula. They simply differed on the likelihood of achieving the projected earnings.

An earn-out may also be used when selling a company. Assume you are trying to sell your business and you and the purchaser do not agree on the value. Suppose that you want to sell a business that you believe is worth $10,000,000, but the potential buyers say it is only worth $5,000,000. You could agree to accept $5,000,000 in cash for the business, but with the condition that you will remain with the company for two years. Then, if you meet certain sales and profit goals during that period, you will receive up to an additional $5,000,000 for the business. If you meet those goals, everyone is happy because of the increased earnings and you have another win-win situation.

What kills more deals than anything else is that people cannot come to an agreement on the value of the company. So why not come to terms on the value later, according to a pre-determined formula? If you are interested and the investor is interested but you do not agree on value, accept their valuation today. But, agree to a sliding-scale or earn-out where the investor agrees to accept your value if you achieve certain financial milestones. Try not to get overly hung up on what you think your business is worth or how much you have to give up. Structure an open-ended deal that will give a good return on money invested and that will leave you with rewards for growing the business. You will be able to close the deal more quickly and the investors will admire your confidence in your ability to achieve. They will have nothing to lose by agreeing to your proposal and you have everything to gain, both in terms of present money invested and in terms of your rewards for leading the growth of the company.

If investors appear interested in your business concept but are not willing to structure a flexible earn-out arrangement with you, be up front with them. Tell them that they appear to want everything at your expense. Tell them that you want a financial business partner. If they do not want to work together so that you are both motivating each other, they can take their money elsewhere, thank you. If you have really sold them on the concept of your investment, you may find that they will come back to you to tell you that they have reconsidered and you can re-open negotiations.

Make sure you understand all the terms and conditions of your contracts with investors. When evaluating financing proposals, the deals may appear extremely complicated. This is not necessarily an indication of financial naiveté of the entrepreneur. Many venture capital deals are difficult for even business and legal professionals to fully comprehend. Seek advice from more than one source. The proposal should be drafted by a lawyer experienced in this area and should be reviewed on your behalf by a business professional experienced in structuring deals.

## *Timing of Additional Financing for an Ongoing Business*

❖ **Make financing the company an ongoing process.**

❖ **Look for financing during the good times, before the business reaches a cash-flow crunch that seriously hinders operations.**

❖ **Use your business plan as a cash-forecasting tool.**

❖ **Look for money as soon as you can factually project increases in sales or when you have achieved a major milestone.**

The timing of additional financing for an on-going business is critical. You do not want to jump the gun and obtain the money too far in advance of when you really need it. To do so may: (1) unnecessarily dilute your equity in the company (by selling stock at too low a valuation because it is still too early for investors to fully value your business) or (2) saddle you with debt obligations (at premium interest rates) before they are needed. Neither do you want to wait until it's too late to raise additional funds. In that event, you may end up with creditors harassing you for payment and an inability to meet the demand for your products and services.

The best way to ensure proper timing of financing is to make financing the company an ongoing process. Develop relationships with potential investors and lenders along the way. Then, when the need for more money arises, you already have established relationships to draw upon. You can educate these potential financiers concerning your company, then give them updates as your financial needs increase and you need to bring in more money. One benefit of forming a company with a business partner, instead of alone, is that one of the partners may concentrate efforts primarily on raising money, while the other partner concentrates on marketing and selling the product or service.

Once a business has become operational, how do you know when is the "right" time to seek additional financing? There is really only one ideal time to raise money for an operational business and that is when everything is going well with the business – when the company looks strong financially and/or when the excitement surrounding the release of the new product is at its peak. At that point, investors are eager to provide funds, and the entrepreneur can afford to be selective about financing terms.

Realistically, however, the entrepreneur is often caught in the difficult position of either trying to raise money too far in advance to support the valuation he or she is seeking for the business, or too late, when there is a cash-flow crunch and the entrepreneur's negotiating posture is seriously hampered. In either instance, the investors, sensing the entrepreneur's predicament but also sensing a potential lucrative return, often try to negotiate a very favorable deal for themselves. The entrepreneur may be forced to accept what seems like an unfair deal in order to meet a cash-flow crisis. Therefore, it is always best to look for financing during the good times, before the business reaches a cash-flow crunch that seriously hinders operations.

It is important to remember that there are two types of cash-flow dilemmas. The most serious is the one caused by excessive overhead (salaries, rent, inventory, etc.) and/or bad accounts receivable without sufficient sales or solid prospects for sales. The other form of cash crisis is caused when a company has strong demand for product and is trying to come up with the money to produce enough product to meet the demand. The entrepreneur generally has an easier time working through the second type of cash-flow crunch than the first. In fact, the second scenario may produce a number of attractive financing opportunities.

Use your business plan as a cash-forecasting tool to help predict your financing needs and to help convince investors to provide the financing you are seeking. Compare the actual performance of your company with the projected performance in your business plan. Make revisions, if necessary, and use the plan to approach financing sources for the money you anticipate needing to fund your continued growth. Your business plan, as previously discussed, should have a series of milestones or goals that you can use to guide and measure your efforts. Your discussions with investors should focus on your performance as measured against these milestones.

If you have a potential big order for your products or services that is likely to increase your production requirements by a substantial percentage, begin to discuss financing with your funding prospects as soon as you sense the order is likely to materialize. Do not wait until the last minute, creating an unnecessary cash and production strain for your company. The time to look for money is as soon as you can factually project increases in sales or when you have achieved a major milestone.

## Using Finders or Brokers

❖ **If you use finders or brokers, clearly spell out the terms of the working relationship from the beginning and stay actively involved throughout the money-raising process.**

Sometimes time constraints or difficulty in obtaining financing may lead to consideration of hiring a finder or broker to put a deal together. Investment bankers, and some lawyers, accountants or other professionals may fulfill such a role.

There are advantages and disadvantages to using finders or brokers to help you find financing. The primary advantage, provided you find a competent resource, is that they can theoretically help you get a higher valuation for your company and, therefore, get a better deal. Also, they can let you devote more of your time to running the business while they are out looking for money. Of course, they do not know your business like you do. You will still have to devote a considerable amount of time to the financing process, but not as much as if you were doing it all yourself.

The primary disadvantage to using finders or brokers is that they will take a cut of the money that you are trying to raise – it will be more expensive. However, in some instances, the savings in time may be well worth the expense.

A finder or broker will probably want the exclusive right to locate your financing. You should try to avoid granting such exclusivity. If you grant exclusivity, grant it for only a limited time and retain the right to seek your own direct sources of funds. Keep in mind that a finder or broker does not have the same vested interest in obtaining the financing (and obtaining it under the best terms) as you do. Therefore, you don't want to cut off all your other options for locating financing.

In theory, you should not need a finder or broker unless all other avenues fail or unless you are trying to buy or sell a business. If you do use finders or brokers, reach a clear understanding about the compensation arrangement from the beginning of the relationship. Ideally, you should not be required to pay a fee or commission until such time as you actually receive funds as a result of the finder/ broker's efforts.

## *Summary Tour*

### FINANCING STRATEGIES

- There is no secret road to successfully raising money.

- The key to succeeding in your quest for funds, no matter what route you choose, is to understand and apply *some basic strategies, then be* creative and persistent.

### *Multiple Sources*

- Approach multiple sources of financing.

- Competition, or at least perceived competition, is the best way to close a deal on the most favorable terms.

- When presenting your concept to investors, realize that not only are you selling the investors on the idea of investing in your company but you are also training them to resell your concept to other investors that they may want to bring into the deal.

- Do not mass-mail your plan to multiple sources.

### *Presentation Hints*

- One of the best shortcuts to obtaining financing is to be organized in your approach to investors.

- Keep your presentation as simple and to-the-point as possible – create excitement and avoid losing your listeners in too many numbers and too much detail.

- End your presentation with a summary of the key points that you want your listeners to remember.

- In following up with an investor, be persistent, but not a pest.

### Good Marketer

- Either be a good marketer of your company or find a business partner or key staff person who can do so.

- A good marketer creates excitement so that people do not feel they are being asked for something but rather are being offered the privilege of participating in a wonderful opportunity.

- Market your business (without lying) so that you are not asking for money but, rather, you are giving the prospective investor the chance to participate in an exciting investment opportunity.

### Positive Attitude

- With prospective investors, always remain confident and positive about yourself, your staff and the business. You are the backbone of the investment that they are considering.

- Once you have your strategy and approach organized, focus your attention on obtaining financing and try to complete the process as quickly as possible.

- Expect rejection initially, but learn from the rejection and always ask for additional leads.

## New v. Tried Concept

- Recognize that financing a business based on a brand new concept is usually more difficult than financing a business in an existing but emerging industry.

## Amount and Type of Financing

- It is often easier to raise large sums of money than it is to raise small sums.

- Try to raise a little more in equity and arrange to borrow a lot more than you think you will need.

## Selection Criteria

- Select investors based not only upon financial considerations but also upon whether or not you will feel comfortable working with them.

- It is better to be a small investment for a large investor than to be a large investment for a small investor.

## *Ongoing Relations With Your Investors*

• Do not promise more to your investors than you can deliver.

### FINANCING PHASES

• Financing a business is usually not a one-time occurrence.

• The financing phases required for a specific business vary depending upon the type of business.

### FINANCING SOURCES

• A key to effectively financing your company is to know which types of sources to approach at which phase of your business development. It is also important to know how to relate to each source.

• Investors in your company, unless they are family and friends, are investing for <u>one</u> reason – they want to make money.

### STRUCTURING THE DEAL

• If possible, tie your financial agreements with investors to the potential growth of your business.

## TIMING OF ADDITIONAL FINANCING FOR AN ON-GOING BUSINESS

• Make financing the company an ongoing process.

• Look for financing during the good times, before the business reaches a cash-flow crunch that seriously hinders operations.

• Use your business plan as a cash-forecasting tool.

• Look for money as soon as you can factually project increases in sales or when you have achieved a major milestone.

## USING FINDERS OR BROKERS

• If you use finders or brokers, clearly spell out the terms of the working relationship from the beginning and stay actively involved throughout the money-raising process.

# Chapter 6

# Moving on Down the Road
## (Sales and Distribution)

## Chapter Destination

*Once you have chosen your destination, planned the itinerary, designed the tour package and arranged to finance the expedition, you are ready to move on down the road with the sale and distribution of your products or services. This chapter presents some guideposts for sales decisions.*

## Distinction Between Sales and Marketing

❖ Selling is the component of marketing that involves the direct contact with the consumer and/or the reseller of your products.

❖ Sales efforts focus on using the best techniques to close the sale of a product or service after the demand or interest has already been created by other marketing factors.

❖ **It is vital to develop a clear sales strategy as part of your overall marketing strategy and to periodically evaluate the effectiveness of that strategy.**

Marketing, which was discussed more fully in chapter 4, "Designing the Tour Package," is a complete system of interacting business activities designed to plan, price, promote, and distribute want-satisfying products and services to present and potential customers. Selling is but one component of marketing. It involves the direct contact with the consumer and/or the reseller of your products. Sales efforts focus on using the best techniques to close the sale of a product after the demand or interest has already been created by other marketing factors.

Sometimes the other aspects of marketing are handled so successfully that selling the product requires little effort. For example, consumable products such as cereal, shampoo and liquor are "sold" primarily through media advertising and through creative and aggressive distribution strategies. Consumers setting out to buy one of these products usually have decided which brand they want to purchase before even entering the store. The decision was made based on the influence of advertisements, other image considerations, or prior use. There is little that needs to be done at the point of sale to influence the purchasing decision, although the location of the product on the shelf or promotional specials may have an impact on the purchasing decision.

On the other hand, other products require much more of a "sales" effort, either to the reseller of the product, to the consumer, or to both. For example, sales of costly products, such as automobiles and computers, depend heavily on the efforts of sales representatives to convince the consumer not only that their product is the best to meet the consumer's wants and needs but also that they are the best retailer from which to purchase.

The cost of goods sold and marketing expenses are the major expenses for many businesses. It is, therefore, vital to develop a clear sales and marketing strategy. Once your business has started operating, it may sometimes be difficult to measure the effectiveness of some of your strategies in generating sales and maximizing profits. Nevertheless, you should take the time to assess which strategies are working, which are not, and why. The successful entrepreneur devotes considerable time not only to creating sales and marketing strategies but also to evaluating their effectiveness.

Key questions to keep in mind in developing a sales strategy are: (1) What are the best sales or distribution channels for your product or service? and (2) How do you make the best use of the channels you have selected? (For example, how do you compensate people?) The rest of this chapter will examine these questions, as well as the question of what to do if you have hit a sales slump.

Although much of the discussion in this chapter is presented from the standpoint of the distribution of a tangible product beginning at the level of the manufacturer, most of the principles also apply to the sale of services and intangible goods at other points in the chain of distribution.

## *Distribution Channels*

❖ **The distribution channels you select for your product or service and your effectiveness in dealing with those channels will determine, to a**

**large degree, the sales volume for your product or service and your profitability.**

❖ **Focus on selecting the distribution channels that will provide the most reliable sales volume first. Build a "core" and protect that core.**

The distribution channels you select for your product or service and your effectiveness in dealing with those channels will determine, to a large degree, the sales volume for your product or service and your profitability.

If you are selling a tangible product or products, distribution options include but are not limited to the following:

• <u>Retail stores</u>. If you sell through retail stores, you have two sales jobs. One is to sell the stores on the idea of carrying your product. The other is to help them sell the product to the consumer. At both levels of sales, there are many questions to resolve. Which types of stores will reach your desired target market niches? Will you sell through smaller, "boutique" types of establishments or through larger department stores? Many stores, particularly in the apparel industry, will not carry a product if certain other stores carry the product because they are trying to preserve a certain image. Will you restrict the type of stores through which you sell your product? Will you sell through discounters? Will you grant protected territories to each retailer that carries your product? Once you know the types of stores that you want to carry your product, how do you convince those stores to stock your product? Will you use distributors, a direct sales force, telemarketing or other methods?

- <u>Mail-order sales</u>. Provided you can locate reliable direct-mail lists of customers who are likely candidates for purchasing your product, mail order may be an extremely effective and comparatively low-cost method of distribution. Mail-order catalogues offer the advantage of allowing the consumer to leisurely browse through the products offered. The shopper can refer back to the catalog multiple times and can take his or her time making the decision to purchase. Mail-order catalogues do not work for all products, though. They work best for products that are not too technical and that have a broad consumer appeal, such as clothing, accessories, books or records.

- <u>Telemarketing</u>. This form of selling is probably the wave of the future, especially with the increasing number of families in which both spouses work outside the home. Telemarketing is an ever-evolving method of distribution. No longer does it just take the form of directly telephoning the consumer or having the consumer telephone to place an order based on newspaper or catalog advertisements. There are, for instance, television stations that demonstrate products that may be ordered over the telephone. Telemarketing, like mail order, is regulated by law to avoid abuse, so you should become familiar with restrictions if you choose this form of distribution.

- <u>Direct sales force</u>. The advantage of hiring an internal, direct sales force is that such a sales force sells only the products of its employer and is under the employer's direct control. The primary disadvantage is that a direct sales force is usually the most expensive way to sell products, at least initially. In the long run, however, a direct sales force may be the least expensive way to sell. As the sales volume increases, the salary and bonuses of a direct sales force may be less than discounts and commissions commanded by independent sales reps, distributors and wholesalers. Depending upon the type of product, using a direct sales force is sometimes the only option. The more technical and expensive a product, the more important it is to have a direct sales force. For example, if the product is a mainframe computer, it is necessary for the person selling the product to be well-versed in the technical qualities and capabilities of the product. The best way to ensure this outcome is to employ a sales force.

- <u>Independent sales representatives</u>. People who act as independent sales representatives provide to the entrepreneur the advantage of an immediate sales force without any up-front expense. Sales reps generally get paid a commission only after they have made a sale. A disadvantage of this option is that the entrepreneur's product will be only one of many sold by the representative. Therefore, the product may not receive the personalized attention that would be given by a direct sales force. A common strategy is to use independent sales reps, initially, and then phase in a direct sales force later. Another strategy is to use the direct sales force for certain key accounts and independent sales representatives for other accounts.

- Distributors/Wholesalers. Some businesses rely almost exclusively on distributors and/or wholesalers to sell their products. This method is most effective when a business is trying to sell small quantities of products to many small retailers. For example, distributors and wholesalers are used extensively in the distribution of microcomputer software and peripherals, books, videos, hardware supplies, and commercial drug and cosmetic products. Typically, a distributor or wholesaler will warehouse substantial quantities of a product, offer the manufacturer a choice of promotional programs, and assume the credit risk with the retailers. Distributors and wholesalers may be more effective than manufacturers in this process because they provide the service for a number of different manufacturers and products, thereby achieving a volume of business with each retailer that makes the distribution process economical and profitable.

The preceding options are not necessarily all of the options available and are not mutually exclusive. You may find that you will use a combination of the distribution channels to most effectively penetrate the market. If you do use more than one distribution channel, it is important to avoid overlapping distribution channels in a way that creates conflicts between the people or organizations selling your product. A disgruntled sales force is not a productive sales force.

Normally, the methodology for selling within an industry becomes standardized as the successful companies all learn the most effective way to distribute their products. In the entrepreneurial stages of an entire industry, however, the entrepreneurs who discover the best distribution methods first are often the big winners. They are the first with the key to penetrating the market most effectively.

In deciding which distribution channels to use, one critical factor is the cost associated with the particular channels. Independent sales representatives may be one of the least expensive ways to sell in the short term. They will only be paid a commission if they sell your product, so your out-of-pocket expenses are low. However, if your product is successful, the commission commanded by the sales rep may exceed amounts that you would pay for other types of sales.

Generally, the most expensive method of sales, especially in the beginning, is the direct sales force. From the time they are hired, the direct sales force will be an expense because the sales people will be receiving a salary and reimbursement for sales expenses. There may be a period of months before a sales person starts generating sufficient sales to cover these expenses. However, there are some products that are most effectively sold through a direct sales force. Also, in the long run, the direct sales force might be better trained, more committed to only your products, capable of generating much higher sales than an independent sales force and, therefore, more economical.

The cost of the product often determines the best method for distributing the product. It is not cost-effective to sell inexpensive products through a direct sales force unless the line of products is very large and the volume very high, which is rare. Usually low-end products will be sold by independent sales representatives, distributors or wholesalers who have other products that can be sold simultaneously to the same buyers.

The expense of the distribution channel is just one factor to consider in selecting methods of distribution. One of the most crucial issues to consider is which channels will provide the greatest exposure to the target market and will generate the most profitable sales mix and volume.

Selection of distribution channels may determine the competitive position of a product in the marketplace. For example, in the wine-cooler industry, one of the first wine cooler companies went from an entrepreneurial start-up operation to first place practically overnight. Then, in a matter of months, the company declined to third place, losing approximately 20% of its market share. The primary reason for this loss of market share was the method of distribution. The company used beer distributors rather than wine distributors, which worked fine for a while. The apparent rationale for this choice was that the company thought wine coolers would compete as much or more with beer than with wine, which was correct. Also, beer distributors visit retail sites more frequently than wine distributors. The problem that resulted was that the company marketed through a variety of competing beer distributors, who often sold to the same stores. The different distributors were then offering different prices and specials for the same product to the same retail establishments, particularly during holidays. This confused the retailers and created competition among the distributors with respect to the product. The opportunity then arose for competitors with more organized distribution methods to surpass the company in sales, even though the company was one of the first on the market with a quality product, a clever name and a successful promotional campaign. Despite these set-backs, however, the company's creative approach to promotion and distribution enabled it to establish a new industry segment and remain a major player (as a division of a larger company).

If your business involves services rather than tangible products, the "distribution channels" may not be as clearly defined as they are for tangible products. Nevertheless, there are some distribution approaches that will be more effective than others, depending upon the type of service you render.

An automobile repair service may find periodic mailers to local area residents offering promotional specials more effective than telemarketing, for example. On the other hand, a moving and storage company may find telemarketing to be the best approach. The company may obtain lists of people who are selling homes and, at this crucial time, may contact such parties by telephone to offer to provide a quote for the move.

Even professions that have not traditionally been thought to use distribution channels are beginning to rely on distribution channels to promote their services as competition for providing those services increases. For example, in the field of medicine, there are now companies (sometimes affiliated with hospitals) that publicly advertise a telephone number to call for referrals to medical doctors. These companies will furnish the names of doctors who provide the type of services the caller is seeking and whose offices are convenient to the caller's location. Sometimes the services will even set up the appointments.

When initially creating your distribution strategy, a key decision must be made. How extensively should you distribute? Should the goal be to get your product on the shelf of every retailer and/or in the catalog of every mail-order establishment or should you be selective? The answer to this question often depends on the nature, price point, and expected sales-life of your product. Typically, the less expensive the product, the broader and less-protected the distribution channels. For less-expensive products, the primary concern may be sales volume. Such products may be marketed through a broad range of resellers, with little thought about selectivity.

In this chapter, we will concentrate more on situations where selectivity is important in choosing distribution channels than where it is not important. We will assume that selectivity is necessary to enhance the image of your product or service and to protect your profit structure. You have decided to limit the number of independent representatives or distributors so that you can better manage your growth, preserve a good reputation and maintain loyalty by preserving attractive profit margins. You know that if everyone sells the product, then competition reduces profitability. Resellers want to sell the product because of its profitability and because of its drawing power for attracting customers who then purchase other products, as well.

Under such circumstances, being selective is important at every level of the distribution process. In selecting distributors and wholesalers, for example, you will want to establish relationships with those most reputable for selling your type of product and having the best contacts with the retailers that you have targeted to carry your product.

If you are selling a product that has some element of uniqueness or exclusivity, you will need to be selective in the number and type of retail establishments through which you sell. Selling the product in several stores within blocks of each other would detract from the uniqueness of the product. To ensure that the stores selected aggressively market your product, you might structure sales quota requirements. Then, if those quotas are not met, you will have the right to market through other establishments.

Selectivity is also important when hiring an internal sales force or contracting with independent sales representatives. The sales skills needed for selling intangible products or services, such as insurance, consulting and advertising services, may differ from the skills required to sell highly technical products, such as mainframe computers and medical equipment. Put yourself in the shoes of the targeted customer and ask yourself what type of salesperson and sales approach would most likely convince you to buy your product. Then look for the people who best meet that description.

When building distribution channels, focus on those that will provide the most reliable sales volume first. Build a "core" and protect that core. Once the core is firmly established, then you can spend a portion of your profits to explore other distribution channels. Never pursue channels that will cut into or destroy your core channels unless you are firmly convinced that the new alternative is better and more profitable.

For example, if the core of your distribution is retail stores and you now want to sell by mail order to customers within the same market area, be sure that you can do so without adversely affecting your relationship with the retailers. If you are a service-provider, such as a consultant, you may have a strong, ongoing relationship with a particular client who refers other clients to you. Before you start marketing your services to a competitor of that client, be sure to take every precaution to protect confidentiality, avoid conflicts of interest and otherwise preserve your relationship with your core client. Preserving the core distribution channels will allow the flexibility to experiment with other marketing approaches without destroying the business.

## Getting the Best Sales Mileage

❖ No matter which sales and distribution channels you use, you will need to take the lead in guiding the sale of your product.

❖ The fewer non-sales-related demands that are placed on your salespeople, the more time they will be able to spend on selling your product or service.

❖ Listen carefully and respond to the feedback your salespeople are getting from customers.

❖ Make profitability, rather than sales volume, your primary sales goal.

❖ Build flexibility into sales commission and compensation packages.

Selecting and establishing sales and distribution relationships are just the first steps in developing a sales strategy. The next step is to figure out how to get the most sales mileage from your chosen channels.

No matter which sales and distribution channels you use, you will need to take the lead in guid-

196 The Entrepreneur's Road Map

ing the sale of your product. How do you want your product presented, to whom, and when?

Even if you are selling through channels other than those that you directly control, you should assume the attitude that all your reseller's sales people are part of your sales force, selling your product. You should tell them how to sell your product. You need to do everything to influence the way the product is sold except give the sales force its pay check. This is another reason why it is important to initially limit distribution of your product, as suggested in the preceding subsection. You need to be able to devote the time and resources to properly training the people in the distribution channel as to how to sell your product. This well-trained core will enable you to more rapidly expand to other channels later.

If you are using an internal, direct sales force, be sensitive to how effectively you are using that sales force to sell your product. A salesperson's job can be more than just closing a sale. For example, you can use your sales force to help with customer service, technical support, collections and deliveries. As we discuss more fully later in this chapter, salespeople need to understand and appreciate the importance of these other functions for making sales and enhancing company profitability. Nevertheless, it is important to remember that the fewer non-sales-related demands that are placed on your salespeople, the more time they will be able to spend on selling your product or service.

One very important rule for getting the most mileage out of sales and distribution channels is to listen carefully and respond to the feedback your salespeople are getting from customers. Salespeople are the real eyes and ears of a company. They have the most customer contact, so they get the most direct customer feedback on the company and its strategies. By listening and responding to that feedback, you can make important adjustments in your product or your sales and marketing strategy that may significantly increase the saleability of your product.

How do you most effectively motivate your salespeople? Commissions and other forms of sales compensation are the most obvious motivators. An entire book could be devoted to the structuring of compensation plans. We will focus on only a few key points to guide you in structuring your own plan.

Sales compensation plans should focus on the complete sales cycle and not just the ordering cycle. Profitability rather than sales volume should be the primary sales goal.

Far too often, salespeople are paid commissions based on orders they take or on orders that have been shipped. Often these commissions are based on the gross sales amount of the orders. Such methods of compensation may be chosen because they are easy to implement and calculate and because they provide an incentive for the salesperson to write as many orders as possible. Often, however, such methods of compensation are not the most beneficial for the company because they make sales volume, rather than profitability, the number one goal.

Far more effective compensation plans focus attention on the entire sales cycle, rather than just the ordering cycle. They take into consideration not only the gross sales amount of the order but also the profitability of the order, delivery of the product, receipt of payment, customer servicing, growth of new business and adjustments for returned goods.

Some ways of building your compensation plans around this broader spectrum of the sales cycle include: (1) Basing the commission on pre-tax profits

198 The Entrepreneur's Road Map

rather than gross sales volume. This produces an incentive for the salesperson to control expenses as well as increase sales volume. (2) Providing that the salesperson will not be paid a commission until the customer has paid for the product. This gives an incentive for sales to credit-worthy customers. (3) Deducting commissions for products which are returned by customers. This discourages sales to customers who are less than serious and gives an incentive for customer follow-up and support. (4) Paying bonuses for sales to existing customers. This focuses attention on building long-term customer relationships.

Cash-poor entrepreneurs quickly see the benefits of compensation plans based on considerations such as those suggested in the preceding paragraph. Such plans focus on open and long-term relationships with customers. They discourage short-term sales gimmicks that might be used by salespeople who are paid based strictly on the number of orders written.

There is usually much more room for structuring creative compensation arrangements with in-house salespeople than with outside sales forces. Independent sales representatives, distributors and wholesalers usually require a commission or discount based on a percentage of sales of the products they sell. There is often little room for negotiating this percentage – it is a "take it or leave it" proposition. The "up side" to the compensation arrangement with such sales forces is that if the sales force does not sell anything, you do not pay anything. If, on the other hand, you have your own direct sales force, you will be paying expenses and a draw against commission even if the sales people have not made any sales.

Try to build flexibility into your agreement with all of your outside sales representatives. You can do this by such strategies as providing that the contract will be renegotiated after a certain period of time or after sales reach a certain level. Whatever arrangement you enter into with sales representatives, try to avoid giving exclusive marketing rights because if you pick a representative that does not produce, you will have strangled the sale of your product. If you are forced to give exclusive rights to a representative that you really believe is the best for your product, set a sales quota. Provide that if that quota is not met, you will have the right to terminate the sales agreement or the exclusivity arrangement. Then you can enter into agreements with other sales representatives.

It is also important to build flexibility into compensation plans for internal direct sales forces. Let the sales people know up front that there may be periodic renegotiations of the compensation package, the sales quotas, the sales territories, etc., as sales progress or as the market changes.

## Sales Slumps

❖ In a sales slump, cut costs in any areas except marketing and sales. Those are the areas that need continued expenditures in order to generate additional sales and revenues.

❖ Analyze why you are in the sales slump so that you will know how to most intelligently spend your sales and marketing dollars.

If you have a product that has been a sales success, but now your sales are sluggish or are declining, what can you do? Most businesses experiencing sales slumps immediately start cutting costs. That is the right thing to do, provided you are cutting costs in the right areas. In a slump, cut costs in any areas except marketing and sales. Those are the areas that need continued expenditures in order to generate additional sales and revenues. Once you pull out of the slump, you can cut back on sales and marketing expenditures and increase expenditures in other areas, such as support services. At that point, you will need to give the best service and support possible to existing customers to generate additional sales through them.

When you are in a sales slump, you can't just blindly continue to pour money into sales and marketing without a logical plan. Obviously, sales and marketing should be scrutinized to eliminate waste, duplication of effort, and other inefficiencies. Also, you will need to analyze why you are in the slump so that you will know how to most intelligently spend your sales and marketing dollars.

Assuming that you were at some point experiencing good sales and then had a decline in sales, you can also assume that something has changed. You have to figure out what has changed so that you will know how to counteract the change to pull sales back up. Has your business changed – the quality of the product, the effectiveness of your compensation package, the abilities of your sales force? If not, has the market changed – has it become saturated with your product; have people's needs changed; is there a new competitor out there? Perhaps the consumers' moods or philosophies have changed. Maybe you are selling desserts but people are now becoming more conscious of their health and weight. They are spending their money on health foods instead of your desserts.

Once you understand the reason for the change in sales, then you will be in a position to decide the best tactic for attacking the problem. In some cases, if the market demand has changed and there is little chance of reversing it, the best decision may be to get into a new business or adopt a new product line that meets the market demand.

## Summary Tour

### DISTINCTION BETWEEN SALES AND MARKETING

- Selling is the component of marketing that involves the direct contact with the consumer and/or the reseller of your products.

- Sales efforts focus on using the best techniques to close the sale of a product or service after the demand or interest has already been created by other marketing factors.

- It is vital to develop a clear sales strategy as part of your overall marketing strategy and to periodically evaluate the effectiveness of that strategy.

### DISTRIBUTION CHANNELS

- The distribution channels you select for your product or service and your effectiveness in dealing with those channels will determine, to a large degree, the sales volume for your product or service and your profitability.

- Focus on selecting the distribution channels that will provide the most reliable sales volume first. Build a "core" and protect that core.

### GETTING THE BEST SALES MILEAGE

- No matter which sales and distribution channels you use, you will need to take the lead in guiding the sale of your product.

- The fewer non-sales-related demands that are placed on your salespeople, the more time they will be able to spend on selling your product or service.

- Listen carefully and respond to the feedback your salespeople are getting from customers.

- Make profitability, rather than sales volume, your primary sales goal.

- Build flexibility into sales commission and compensation packages.

### SALES SLUMPS

- In a sales slump, cut costs in any areas except marketing and sales. Those are the areas that need continued expenditures in order to generate additional sales and revenues.

- Analyze why you are in the sales slump so that you will know how to most intelligently spend your sales and marketing dollars.

# Chapter 7

## Staying on Course
### (Managing the Business)

### Chapter Destination

*Creating the business is just the beginning of the entrepreneur's journey. Once created, the business must be steered and guided on the course mapped by the entrepreneur. This chapter presents keys to successfully navigating the management of the business.*

## Meaning of Management

❖ **Management is leading and inspiring people to achieve their best as individuals and to work together as a team to accomplish the goals and objectives of a business.**

Managing a business calls for an entirely different focus and set of skills than those required for creating and developing the business idea. Successful management depends upon both the personal qualities of the manager and the management techniques employed. This chapter presents a view of both, as well as hints for selecting and structuring agreements with management team members.

It is very important to adopt a particular management philosophy for your company to follow. Following a specific philosophy promotes uniform and consistent management. The uniformity and consistency serve as a stabilizing force for the business and lead to more systematic, effective decision-making. Your company's management philosophy might be based on one or a combination of management theories – whatever best suits you and your situation.

The real meaning of the word, "management," often becomes obscured by the many theories, styles and principles that have been touted, from time to time, as the best way to manage a business. You hear about management by consensus, management by objective, management by exception and management by motivation, to name just a few. These are all valid and effective methods of management. We will discuss some of them later in this chapter.

The most important thing to remember, however, no matter which management style you adopt, is the real meaning of management. Management is the ability to lead and inspire people to achieve their best as individuals and to work together as a team to accomplish the goals and objectives of a business.

## Qualities of Successful Managers/Leaders

❖ **Successful managers/leaders:**

- **Exercise sound business judgment**
- **Possess self-confidence**
- **Exhibit consistency**

- Communicate clearly and openly – which means they really LISTEN
- Demonstrate respect and support for employees
- Create an atmosphere of teamwork
- Lead by example
- Understand their own strengths and weaknesses.

The best managers perceive themselves and are perceived by those they manage as leaders. The success of a leader depends upon the support of the followers. To be supportive, the followers must feel confident that they are being led down a path to success and must feel comfortable entrusting their careers to the leader. The qualities described in this subsection inspire the trust, confidence and comfort necessary to make managers successful.

### *Sound Business Judgment*

Those being led and managed must believe in the good judgment of their leader before they will trust and follow that leader. They must have confidence that business decisions will be based on well-reasoned business considerations rather than on erratic, emotional responses.

Sound business judgments result from gathering as much reliable and competent information as possible concerning each business issue and then basing decisions on the course of action that will most effectively accomplish the goals and objectives of the business. Prior to making a decision concerning a particular issue, a good leader will solicit information and opinions from employees who have knowledge that is relevant to the issue. This gives employees a better understanding of the issues facing the leader, a sense of participating in the decision, and a feeling that the leader is making decisions through careful consideration rather than through impulse. No doubt, many of the best leaders often rely on "gut level" responses in making decisions rather than on a detailed logical analysis. Nevertheless, effective "gut level" impulses are based on a clear understanding of the issues and the goals of the company.

### _Self-confidence_

The more managers believe in and have confidence in themselves, the more others will have confidence in them. A manager who lacks genuine self-confidence may have difficulty making and standing by decisions, which will undermine such manager's perceived leadership abilities. Also, managers who lack self-confidence or self-esteem may be reluctant to hire qualified support staff for fear the followers will outshine the leader. They may withhold rewards or give excessive negative feedback to those they manage so that they will appear inferior to the manager.

The best managers are those who feel so good about themselves that they are not threatened by the strengths of those they lead. They realize that the better their followers look and perform, the more successful the company will be and, therefore, the better the leader will look.

### _Consistency_

By being consistent, good leaders make it easy for others to follow their lead. One of the greatest frustrations to employees is to try to follow a leader who is constantly changing goals and directions or

who praises a particular behavior one day and repri-
mands it another day. Inconsistent managers will
soon find that they are not respected or viewed as
leaders by those they manage.

A flaw in many entrepreneurs is that they want
to be too dictatorial and make all of the decisions.
What may then happen is that the entrepreneur
makes an "off the cuff" decision without taking the
time to really think through the issues. Then, later,
the entrepreneur discovers information that should
have been gathered before the decision was made and
ends up changing the decision. There is nothing
wrong with changing a decision. If changes happen
too often, however, employees will be reluctant to
enthusiastically follow the direction set by the entrepreneur for fear the entrepreneur will change course
in mid-stream. One key to maintaining consistency is
to make decisions based on the best available data
and to involve others in decisions so that they will
understand and support decisions, as suggested in the
section above on sound business judgment.

### Communication Skills

Good communication skills are absolutely essential to good management. The manager must effectively communicate the goals and priorities of the
company to those being managed so they will clearly
understand what they must do to promote the company's success. Effective communication of company
goals is fostered by keeping those goals as simple as
possible and by repeating them often so that they stay
in the forefront of employees' minds. Another extremely effective way to communicate goals, besides
repetition, is to tie compensation to the accomplishment of certain goals.

Communication is a two-way process. It is important for a manager to promote feedback from employees. The best way to do this is to really listen and respond to such feedback. Informal discussions, such as one-on-one or small-group lunch meetings, or regularly-scheduled staff meetings are effective for soliciting and responding to communication from employees, as well as for keeping employees advised about company goals and accomplishments. Feedback from sales and marketing staff is particularly important because they are the people who have the most direct contact with customers. A company must be responsive to its customers, and therefore must listen to the staff members who have the closest contact with those customers.

### *Respect and Support for Employees*

Managers obtain optimal performance from employees if they: (1) select the best candidates for positions; (2) clearly communicate the goals of the company and expectations for the position; (3) trust and respect the skills and abilities of those they have selected; (4) structure goals that are attainable so that employees may experience successes rather than constant frustration from non-attainment of goals; (5) effectively praise and reward successful performance by employees; and (6) provide criticism in a constructive manner. As pointed out in an earlier section of this chapter, the more self-confidence and self-esteem a manager has, the easier it will be for that manager to accomplish these goals.

Most people want to feel self-esteem and a sense of accomplishment, particularly in their careers. Most employees who sense the respect of their leaders and who feel that they are being depended upon to perform important tasks for the business will be motivated to prove that the respect is deserved and that they are capable of meeting expectations.

Setting goals that are attainable and rewarding high-quality job performance promote employee self-esteem and motivate employees to continue such performance. Rewards may be as simple as a word of praise or recognition or may take the form of bonuses, prizes or promotions for achieving certain goals.

Effectively guiding employee performance requires giving constructive criticism of areas needing change as well as rewards for desired performance. If criticism is offered in a respectful and positive way, it may be appreciated by employees and viewed as a learning experience One of the best ways to offer constructive criticism is to schedule regular reviews of employee performance during which employees expect impartial and constructive review of both their strong points and areas that may need improvement. Another advantage of such regular reviews is that they also provide an opportunity to receive feedback from employees about management practices or other areas of the business that may need improvement.

### *Creating an Atmosphere of Teamwork*

The road to a company's success will be much smoother if there is a spirit of teamwork and pulling together, rather than separatism and infighting among the employees and divisions of the company. Effective leaders promote teamwork by: (1) making sure that the objectives of the various departments and positions are consistent and not contradictory, (2) selecting management team members who are compatible and (3) making sure that the members of the different divisions of the company understand each other's goals and objectives. The key to promoting such an understanding is to have good systems of communication, such as periodic meetings of department heads and other forms of intra-office communications.

One of the most important areas in which to promote teamwork is the budget-setting process. Assuming that the goal of a company is to increase income and control expenses, one of the best ways to ensure that key managers support this goal is to make them a part of the budget decision-making process. Managers who understand the basis for financial decisions and who have input into those decisions will think more like the president of the company. They will more naturally pull together toward common business goals rather than trying solely to protect their own management division.

### *Leading by Example*

The successful leader ensures that management goals and policies are carried out both by setting an example and by follow-through. A manager who says that one of the company's goals is to drastically reduce unnecessary expenses and who then charters an airplane at the company's expense for an extravagant weekend trip to the Mardi Gras will not inspire cost-cutting among support staff. To be effective, a manager must practice what he or she preaches.

Company goals and policies mean little unless managers take steps to see that these goals and policies are followed. The help of a good human resources person or department is often invaluable for follow-through. Typically, a company can afford such human resources staff sooner than the entrepreneur realizes. The entrepreneur may not always see the hidden costs of ineffective leadership and lack of enforcement of company policy. Ask employees in a successful company what the company's goals are or when and how the salary review process works. Those employees will know the answers to those questions and the answers will be consistent. Ask the same questions in a less successful company and you will often get confusing and conflicting answers.

### Understanding Personal Strengths and Weaknesses

To fully gain the support and respect of those they lead, it is important for managers/leaders to show a clear understanding of their own strengths and weaknesses. Leaders who are capable of open and honest self-analysis inspire open communication from their followers. Other people develop confidence in the decision-making abilities of leaders who are not blind to their own weaknesses and who understand their own strengths.

## Management Techniques

❖ Some key elements of effective management are:

- Keeping all aspects of management as simple as possible
- Clearly defining the goals and objectives of the business ("Management by Objective")
- Narrowing of the focus of what is being managed ("Management by Exception")

- Interacting with employees and co-workers in a manner that motivates and inspires top-level performance and teamwork ("Management by Motivation")
- Periodically reviewing and refining goals, objectives, priorities and motivational incentives
- Selecting people whose abilities are a good match for each position and who are compatible with each other.

## *Keep It Simple*

Often, one of the best principles for effectively managing a business, no matter what management style you use, is the KIS principle – Keep It Simple. Applying the KIS principle becomes more difficult as the business grows and becomes more complex. Nevertheless, in the beginning phases of a business, there are usually limited layers of management, limited amounts of time and more work than there are hands or brains to accomplish it. At that point, especially, it is absolutely necessary to keep it simple and to set priorities for what has to be done.

Confronted with more issues than they have time and people to deal with, successful entrepreneurs stay on course by having a very clear idea of the critical functions in each area of the business and the priorities of those functions. The more simply stated they are, the easier they are to keep in mind and follow. By focusing attention on those critical functions and priorities, the entrepreneur can more easily see the important goals through all the competing input. Successful entrepreneurs do only what has to be done to accomplish their goals. They are adept at staying on course by keeping things simple and keeping their attention focused.

## *Management by Objective*

One of the keys to effectively managing a company is to have clearly defined goals and objectives for the company and for each person and department of the company. These goals and objectives should be defined before you begin to hire people. The essence of making wise hiring decisions is to hire the best people to accomplish your objectives.

What dollar volume of your various products and services do you want to sell over the next three years; to which target markets; using what type of sales approach? What objectives must each division adopt to meet your overall company goals? Objectives of the different divisions must be consistent with each other and supportive of overall company goals. Then you will not end up with two divisions fighting against each other because they have contradictory goals.

To illustrate, assume that through your budgeting process it was determined that your company's overall sales goal for the year is $10,000,000. Your objectives and the parameters for achieving them are: (1) to derive 75% of these sales through domestic sources and 25% through foreign sources; (2) to sell 60% through direct channels and 40% through wholesalers; (3) to keep the cost of goods sold under 30% of sales; (4) to limit sales and marketing expenses to no more than 20% of sales; (5) to achieve pre-tax profits of 10%; (6) to raise no additional equity ; and (7) to establish a line of credit equal to 80% of accounts receivable with a $3,000,000 limit. Every person in every department of your company should be informed that these are the company's objectives and the parameters under which to achieve them. Then the managers of each department should work together to set goals for their own departments to accomplish these overall company objectives.

Sales and marketing departments should plan strategies to reach the customers and distributors necessary to meet the goals. Similarly, the finance department should manage cash and the manufacturing department should manage purchasing and production in sufficient volumes and according to the timetables necessary to fill the orders generated by sales and marketing.

Far too often, companies are said to have failed to achieve their goals because one or more of the functional areas "messed up." In reality, top management "messed up" for not making sure that the team had coordinated compatible strategies to accomplish the goals and objectives of the company.

### Management by Exception

Management by exception means setting priorities and establishing routines for recurring tasks or situations. This minimizes the number of decisions that must be made and frees managers to focus on exceptional decisions and issues.

Routines or procedures conserve time. Making a decision requires time and energy. Rather than consume time to make a new decision each time a recurring task is called for, time may be used more economically by establishing a procedure for performing that task. That task can then be performed in the future with a minimal expenditure of time. Decision-making time will then be required for that task only when unusual or exceptional circumstances arise.

Often, too much management time is spent on routine decisions and not enough time on the critical areas needed to expand the business. Successful entrepreneurs try to keep the attention of management staff focused on the real issues by having the more routine, recurring functions handled by non-management personnel. This requires the entrepreneur to set clear objectives and priorities and to demand that managers effectively organize their areas.

### *Management by Motivation*

It is relatively easy to establish business goals and objectives. However, unless people are continually reminded what those goals and objectives are, efforts will get dispersed and the business will not operate as efficiently and as profitably as possible. That is why it is important to build into the management process motivational factors that will constantly remind people of the important goals of the company. Using management by motivation will keep the business operating in line with your major objectives and goals.

How do you motivate people? One of the most effective methods is to motivate with money. Tie compensation packages to key items that will motivate. A side benefit of keeping motivational rewards as a major part of compensation packages is that doing so keeps a large portion of salary expense variable. This can be very helpful to a small, growing company.

Incentive compensation is fairly easy to structure for sales people. As discussed more fully in chapter 6, you can simply provide for a base salary plus a commission equal to a percentage of the sales or profits generated by the sales person. Although it is sometimes not as simple to structure incentive compensation in non-sales areas, there are usually ways to arrange such structures. In a purchasing department, for example, you might establish a compensation package with 50% consisting of a fixed salary of X dollars and the other 50% being a bonus based on achieving a specific inventory turnover and profit-margin level. In the collections department, perhaps the incentive is tied to keeping accounts receivable to a certain number of days outstanding or less. For example, for every day accounts receivable average less than 45 days outstanding, a dollar amount equal to a percentage of the interest saved can be set aside for bonuses.

The management or executive staff should be compensated according to a flexible compensation plan under which a base salary is supplemented with an aggressive bonus package. For example, the base salary could be kept at around 50% of the projected compensation. The remaining compensation could be paid in the form of a bonus based mainly on profits, with perhaps a lesser portion based on the manager's specific departmental responsibility.

Incentive compensation should also be implemented for lower levels of the organization. However, it is important to realize that employees with lower compensation should probably have a smaller portion of their compensation in the form of incentives. The incentive portion should probably be 10-25% of compensation so that those employees have sufficient base earnings to cover cost-of-living expenses.

## *Reviewing and Revising Management Goals*

It is best to review management goals, objectives, priorities and motivational incentives on a periodic basis to be sure that they and your business are in line with each other as the business grows and develops. You may find it necessary to revise them every year or six months to keep the business on track.

Naturally, goals and priorities will change as the business grows. Such changes are best handled in a way that is perceived by employees as positive, rather than negative. Many employees look for stability and find change threatening. Talk of changing incentive-compensation plans may be particularly threatening because such changes may reduce the amount of money that the employee can expect to make.

The best way to handle change is to communicate. Employees should be led to understand, from the beginning, that the business is growing. Explain that changes will occur in response to such growth and changing market conditions. Let employees know that you will be reviewing and revising the goals, objectives, priorities and incentive compensation plans of the business on a periodic basis. Then, follow through with such review and revision. Involve key employees in the planning and budgeting cycle so that they understand why particular changes are being made.

## *Selecting the Management Team*

The starting point for making a hiring decision is to assess what attributes and skills the position requires in order to best meet the goals and objectives of the company. The next step is to find the person who possesses these attributes and skills and whose

218 The Entrepreneur's Road Map

personal goals mesh with those of the company. When hiring managers, it is also important to find people who possess the leadership qualities described earlier in this chapter.

The managers to hire are those who have the ability and the mental stability to stay level-headed when all about them there is a war going on or there is a fire needing to be extinguished. Choose those who have the ability to concentrate on the three or four most important issues and yet have a good enough understanding of the job to know the effect of the things on which they are not focusing. Another crucial characteristic to look for in managers is the ability to clearly communicate the company priorities to those who are being managed.

When you hire, hire the best people you can for each position at each different phase of the business. Hire somebody equal to or better than yourself. Sometimes, managers want to perpetuate their power and therefore hire people with lesser skills than themselves. Do not fall into that trap. It only weakens the company. Make hiring decisions that will make the company strong. One way to promote hiring the best candidate for a position is to make hiring a group decision. When hiring key managers, have them interviewed by all of the key functional managers with whom they will be working.

Do not hire someone based solely on that person's reputation. Make sure the prospective employee really believes in your objectives. Find out if the candidate demonstrates genuine excitement for your business ideas and direction. The type of person you should seek for each of your functional areas is someone who is enthusiastic about your business and who understands and agrees with your business objectives.

You do not necessarily want the best person for running a billion-dollar company when you plan on having a two-million-dollar company. If you select the person running the billion-dollar company, that person will be accustomed to managing complex budgets and other complicated systems that are not applicable to your operation. For your two-million-dollar company, you want a person who is bright, aggressive and still willing to do "hands on" management. You want a person with good talents and management skills – someone who is willing to work long and hard to do a lot of the work himself or herself, knowing that if he/she succeeds, the company will succeed and he or she will later have a staff of people to handle many of the business details. The person selected should have some risk-taking orientation and not just be concerned about a nice office and a good compensation package.

When you are selecting key employees, not only are you selecting the people with the best talents for the positions, but you are also selecting members of a team. Therefore, it is important to be sure that your key employees are compatible. Key employees must work together toward the common goal of a successful business. If they are incompatible, too much energy will be drained by conflict and political posturing. This will be detrimental to the business. We do not mean to imply that you should expect a conflict-free working environment. There will always be some conflict – in fact, a degree of conflict or competition can be positive and stimulating. You must, however, have people who are willing to work together to resolve conflict and who let the larger goals of the business override their own personal conflicts or competitiveness with other staff members.

Different people are right for key positions at different phases of the business. Management styles and philosophies will change as the company grows. In the growth stages of the business, you need key employees who are somewhat entrepreneurial, creative types; who do not mind taking the risk with you that your business will succeed; and who believe in their own abilities to help build the business. Once the business has become well-established, the types of talents needed to run the business may differ. You may need more organizationally-driven, administrative types rather than the entrepreneurial types who helped start the business.

The fact that you will need different types of people at different phases of the business does not mean that you should get rid of the people who helped build the business. It just means that as you add layers of managers and replace people who leave, you may need to focus on different talents. You may want to let your managers know up front that other senior-level managers will be added at later stages of the business. That way, you avoid creating the feeling among hardworking managers that they are being overlooked or punished in some way when a new employee is hired later in a higher level position. One way to make room for additional management layers at later phases of the company is with titles – for example, on your organizational chart, you may have titled slots for positions that you intend to fill later that are above the titles of the people you are currently hiring. That way, you can bring in additional managers later without having to demote someone who is already working for the company.

## *Agreements With Key Employees*

❖ **Agreements with key employees should be structured both to provide performance incentives for the employee, such as profit sharing or stock ownership, and to protect the company in the event the relationship terminates.**

An excellent way to promote high achievement and teamwork among key employees is to provide opportunities for those key employees to benefit from the growth of the company through participation in profits, bonuses, and/or through ownership of stock or stock options. These types of benefits are in some ways similar to the incentive compensation discussed previously under the subsection "Management by Motivation." They are also different in that they are tied to the overall performance of the company rather than to the performance of specific functional objectives.

While it is important for key employees to have some sort of profit- or equity-participation in the company, it is also important to structure protections for the company in the event the relationship terminates. Some of the selected key employees will not work out. Recognizing this to be true, agreements that are structured with key employees should provide for clean breaks if the relationship terminates. This will help avoid long, legal battles and time-consuming discussions at the time the break occurs. Companies have become involved in lawsuits that have dragged on for months and years just because the parties did not take the time to structure the proper employment agreements at the beginning of the relationship. The agreements do not have to be fancy and complicated. They should take the common-sense approach that if the relationship works, this is what the employee can expect to receive, but if the relationship does not work, this is how we part company.

Some protections for the company that may be built into employment agreements are: (1) requirements that the employee must work with the company for a specified period of time before profit-sharing or equity-participation rights begin to vest; (2) the protection and non-disclosure of trade secrets, patents, and other confidential and proprietary information of the company; (3) non-competition clauses (although these must be narrowly written to be enforceable); (4) the reacquisition of stock by the company in the event the employee's employment is terminated; and (5) the rights, if any, of the employee to severance pay or ongoing commissions from sales made prior to termination.

## Summary Tour

### MEANING OF MANAGEMENT

- Management is leading and inspiring people to achieve their best as individuals and to work together as a team to accomplish the goals and objectives of a business.

### QUALITIES OF SUCCESSFUL MANAGERS/LEADERS

Successful managers/leaders:

- Exercise sound business judgment
- Possess self-confidence

- Exhibit consistency
- Communicate clearly and openly – which means they really LISTEN
- Demonstrate respect and support for employees
- Create an atmosphere of teamwork
- Lead by example
- Understand their own strengths and weaknesses

## MANAGEMENT TECHNIQUES

Some key elements of effective management are:

- Keeping all aspects of management as simple as possible
- Clearly defining the goals and objectives of the business ("Management by Objective")
- Narrowing of the focus of what is being managed ("Management by Exception")
- Interacting with employees and co-workers in a manner that motivates and inspires top-level performance and teamwork ("Management by Motivation")
- Periodically reviewing and refining goals, objectives, priorities and motivational incentives
- Selecting people whose abilities are a good match for each position and who are compatible with each other.

## AGREEMENTS WITH KEY EMPLOYEES

- Agreements with key employees should be structured both to provide performance incentives for the employee, such as profit sharing or stock ownership, and to protect the company in the event the relationship terminates.

# Chapter 8

## Tour Guides
### (Working With Business Advisors)

### Chapter Destination

*Just as tour guides may help travellers find the best routes, avoid pitfalls, and derive the most benefit from their journeys, so may business advisors, if used properly, facilitate the entrepreneur's business journey. This chapter provides guidance for selecting and deriving the most benefit from business advisors.*

## Selecting Business Advisors

❖ When selecting a business advisor, consider the following :

- Is the advisor experienced in the area in which you need assistance?
- Are the rates charged by the advisor reasonable?

- Do you feel comfortable that the prospective advisor exercises sound business judgment and relates well with you and your company representatives who will be interacting with the advisor?

❖ Set priorities for the areas in which you feel you need advice.

❖ Determine whether a particular need would best be served by hiring a full- or part-time employee rather than an independent consultant.

❖ Avoid advisors who do not admit areas of strength and weakness and who learn at your expense.

Starting and operating a business requires multiple talents and skills. The entrepreneur is called upon to perform a variety of functions – business planning, marketing, selling, legal compliance, management, accounting, etc. Very few entrepreneurs are experts in all of these areas. The wise entrepreneur acknowledges the areas in which the business would benefit from the assistance of other people – either employees, business partners, or outside consultants – and then finds the best people to provide the needed services. Relationships with employees and business partners are discussed in other chapters of this road map. This chapter will focus on selecting and working with independent business advisors.

There are countless business advisors who are more than willing to assist with most any aspect of starting and operating a business. Attorneys, accountants, business consultants, management consultants, investment/financial advisors, insurance agents, marketing consultants, independent sales representatives and many other categories of business advisors make their living by providing advice and assistance to businesses.

When selected and used properly, independent business advisors may immeasurably accelerate and enhance the success rate of a business. On the other hand, if the wrong advisors are chosen for particular tasks or if the chosen advisors are not managed properly by the entrepreneur, the results may be disastrous. Such errors may steer the business completely off track, result in expenditures far in excess of the value of the services provided, or even contribute to the failure of the business.

When selecting a business advisor, consider the following: (1) Is the advisor experienced in the area in which you need assistance? Ask for references. (2) Are the rates charged by the advisor reasonable? and (3) Do you feel comfortable that the prospective advisor exercises sound business judgment and relates well with you and your company representatives who will be interacting with the advisor?

The entrepreneur starting a business may feel that there are many areas in which he or she needs assistance from advisors. As with all aspects of business, it then becomes necessary to set priorities. What are the areas in which you most need assistance? Which areas of advice will help you improve your bottom line by increasing sales or decreasing expenses? What do you need to know to protect yourself from penalties or fines, keep you out of jail, and protect yourself from costly lawsuits?

Once you have identified an area in which you need assistance, the first question to consider is whether that need would best be served by hiring a full- or part-time employee rather than an independent consultant. If the area is one that will require concentrated attention over a long period of time, it may be more economical to hire someone. The hourly rate of independent consultants is generally much higher than the per-hour rate of an employee, because consultants are charging enough to cover their overhead and profit.

If you have decided that a task requires the services of an outside advisor, select someone who is experienced in the specific area of need. Avoid advisors who do not admit areas of strengths and weakness and who learn at your expense. For example, if you want to raise money through a private placement, seek legal counsel experienced in securities law. If you select an attorney who is not experienced in this area, you will probably end up paying more than you would for an experienced attorney because you will be paying for the time required for the inexperienced attorney's research. Also, experience brings with it knowledge of time-saving shortcuts, an ability to quickly judge what is and is not important, and a refinement of technique. The volume of information in our society is impossible for any one person to master. Therefore, advisors must necessarily specialize and cannot be all things to all people. Take the time to find the advisor with the right background for your needs.

You may wish to select some advisors who are generalists, who will refer you to specialists when necessary. Just be sure that advisors selected to fill this role are people who will not hesitate to admit areas that are outside of their expertise and who will be willing and able to refer you to the appropriate specialists, when necessary. The advantage of this approach is to have one advisor who is familiar with your overall business operations and needs, who can be consulted as needed concerning questions that arise from time to time and who can serve as a resource for referrals.

As you are planning your business or making major changes, we strongly recommend consulting with general business advisors, such as accountants and attorneys experienced in working with businesses and familiar with your business. They may provide invaluable guidance that will steer you onto the proper course and help avoid costly mistakes and changes.

Business advisors are also very useful for setting up systems, performing periodic checks of those systems, and providing advice on an "as needed" basis. The actual administration and implementation of the systems set up by business advisors are then usually handled most economically by employees. For example, if your business requires the development of a specialized computer system for tracking orders and keeping records, you may wish to retain an independent computer consultant to set up the system you need. Once the system is set up, you may need to retain that consultant to periodically maintain the system, answer questions, or provide training, but the actual use of the system may best be handled by your own employees trained in the use of the system.

It is important for you to feel comfortable with the advisor you have selected. You should feel confident that the advisor is knowledgeable, exercises sound business judgment and relates well with you and your company representatives who will be interacting with the advisor. Also, you should believe that the rates charged are reasonable.

## Working with Business Advisors

❖ Business advisors may be managed most effectively by:

- Clearly identifying and defining the tasks needing the advice of outside advisors
- Clearly communicating the tasks to the advisor
- Requesting an advance estimate of the amount of time and money required to perform the task
- Insisting that the advisor establish milestones by which you can regularly monitor his or her progress toward the agreed-upon goal
- Requesting that the advisor inform you if, at any point, he or she sees that the actual cost of performing the task may exceed the original estimate
- Signing a written agreement that clearly addresses the points raised above and other terms and conditions of the relationship.

When working with independent advisors, keep in mind their perspective. They want to help your business, but they are in business, too. The more time they spend helping you, the more they earn and the more you spend. For that reason, the entrepreneur needs to know how to manage the use of such advisors.

Business advisors may be managed most effectively by: (1) clearly identifying and defining the tasks needing the advice of outside advisors; (2) clearly communicating the tasks to the advisor; (3) requesting an advance estimate of the amount of time and money required to perform the task; (4) insisting that the advisor establish milestones by which you can regularly monitor his or her progress toward the agreed-upon goal; (5) requesting that the advisor inform you if, at any point, he or she sees that the actual cost of performing the task may exceed the original estimate; and (6) signing a written agreement that clearly addresses the points raised above and other terms and conditions of the relationship.

Demanding accountability through measurable milestones is mandatory to properly manage a consultant. The milestones can range from weekly reports that not only summarize progress but also include an estimate of time and resources needed to complete the task, to a project management system with predefined tasks and estimated hours for each task. Any number of written methodologies will work – the key is to demand periodic written performance reports, together with an estimate for completion.

The fees of independent advisors are usually based on one or a combination of the following four arrangements: the flat fee, the hourly fee, the percentage fee or the contingency fee.

The **flat fee** basis of compensation simply means that you will be charged a specified amount for receiving a particular service. If you are being charged a flat fee, just be sure to clarify exactly what is included. For example, a fee quoted by an attorney for establishing a corporation probably includes just the preparation of the articles of incorporation, by-laws and organizational minutes. Your corporation may also need a stockholders' agreement, key employee agreement or other legal documents for which you will be separately charged.

Under an **hourly fee** arrangement, you will be charged a specific hourly rate for services rendered. If you are using a large firm, the hourly rate will vary depending upon the individual who performs particular services. For instance, in a large law firm, an attorney responsible for coordinating a particular project may charge a rather high hourly rate. That attorney may then assign actual research, drafting or other ministerial duties to paralegals or junior attorneys whose hourly rates are less expensive. The hourly fee arrangement often leads to surprisingly large bills for clients who have not spelled out fee limits for the advisor performing the service. Most advisors who charge on an hourly basis are more than willing to work with the client to establish a cap on the amount that will be charged for a particular service. Do not be shy about clarifying amounts to be charged or about questioning a bill that you believe is excessive. You should feel comfortable that you are getting your money's worth from business advisors.

In some instances, a **percentage fee** may be charged. For example, if you use the services of a broker or finder to help locate sources of financing, you may be charged a percentage of funds raised. If this is the type of fee arrangement, clarify that the fee will be paid when funds are actually received and not before. If you receive the financing in stages, you may also wish to pay the fee in proportionate stages.

Occasionally, a third-party service provider may charge a **contingent fee**. Under this arrangement, you only pay if the provider achieves a certain result. For example, a collection agency or a litigator may, in some circumstances, charge a fee only for amounts collected. Usually, the contingency fee is based on a percentage of amounts recovered. The percentage may seem high. That is because the service provider is assuming the risk of putting in time for which no payment will be received if no amounts are collected. The benefit is that you do not have to pay unless amounts are recovered for your benefit.

Sometimes combinations of the above fee arrangements are used. To illustrate, an attorney may accept a case on a contingent-fee basis, but with the stipulation that you will pay a specified fixed fee or hourly rate if you drop the case before it is litigated or settled. An example that combines elements of the fixed fee and hourly fee arrangements are counselors who suggest a retainer arrangement. Under this arrangement, you pay a specified dollar amount per month for the right to call upon the counselor for advice. For you, the advantage of this arrangement is that you are guaranteed the ability to call upon the advisor for up to a specified number of hours of advice each month. Also, the billing rate may be less than if you did not have a retainer agreement. The disadvantage is that you are paying the money, whether or not you are using the service. The fact that you do not use up the time allotted to you during a particular month usually does not allow you to use that time in a subsequent month.

You may find in working with a business advisor that you can save money and achieve better results by performing parts of a task yourself. For instance, if you have retained a consultant to assist with preparing your business plan, you should prepare a first draft of the plan, yourself, according to an outline or guidelines provided by your advisor. Not only might you save money by doing so but also, more importantly, you will be forced to think through the goals and directions of your company and make decisions affecting your company's growth.

## *Summary Tour*

### SELECTING BUSINESS ADVISORS

- When selecting a business advisor, consider the following:

  - Is the advisor experienced in the area in which you need assistance?
  - Are the rates charged by the advisor reasonable?
  - Do you feel comfortable that the prospective advisor exercises sound business judgment and relates well with you and your company representatives who will be interacting with the advisor?

- Set priorities for the areas in which you feel you need advice.

- Determine whether a particular need would best be served by hiring a full- or part-time employee rather than an independent consultant.

- Avoid advisors who do not admit areas of strength and weakness and who learn at your expense.

### WORKING WITH BUSINESS ADVISORS

Business advisors may be managed most effectively by:

- Clearly identifying and defining the tasks needing the advice of outside advisors

- Clearly communicating the tasks to the advisor
- Requesting an advance estimate of the amount of time and money required to perform the task
- Insisting that the advisor establish milestones by which you can regularly monitor his or her progress toward the agreed-upon goal
- Requesting that the advisor inform you if, at any point, he or she sees that the actual cost of performing the task may exceed the original estimate.
- Signing a written agreement that clearly addresses the points raised above and other terms and conditions of the relationship.

# Chapter 9

## Avoiding Detours
### (Anticipating and Avoiding Obstacles)

### Chapter Destination

*One of the great entrepreneurial tragedies occurs when the long-struggling entrepreneur finally starts to see the fruits of his or her efforts, but then takes a detour that causes the business to fail or prolongs the attainment of success. This chapter provides cautions and warning signals for road hazards that may throw the entrepreneur off track.*

## Imagined versus Real Success

❖ One of the most common detours for the entrepreneur is to mistake imagined success for real success.

❖ Measures of success include:

- Industry comparisons
- Cash reserves

- **Sales base**
- **Profit levels**
- **Response of financiers**
- **Achievement of business-plan goals**

One of the most common detours for the entrepreneur is to mistake imagined success for real success. Entrepreneurs who prematurely think they have succeeded may begin to divert CASH and TIME elsewhere. This may occur just at the time when it is most important to invest almost all their money and time back into the business to strengthen it so that it will continue to grow.

Business magazines frequently feature lists of the privately-held or small, publicly-held companies with the top annual sales volume or fastest growth in annual sales. If you follow these lists from year to year, you will note that companies that were on the list one year may have disappeared from the list in a subsequent year. The companies that have disappeared typically had good business concepts and appeared to be making money.

What could have caused these shooting stars of business to fall? Frequently, the cause of the decline was that the entrepreneurs mistook imagined success for real success. Perhaps they became overconfident, and began to divert time and money away from the core business, only to find out a short time later that these mistakes have come back to haunt them. The businesses no longer appear among the published lists of successes. In many cases, the businesses are still operational and the entrepreneurs still have the chance to fight back toward success again. In other less fortunate cases, however, the businesses have gone bankrupt or have folded.

The lesson to be learned is that a business can decline or disappear very quickly, even though it appears to have achieved success. The way to avoid such a hazard is to achieve real rather than imagined success. Imagined success is a first level of apparent success for the entrepreneur who has been struggling to achieve a consistent cash flow. Entrepreneurs who have reached this stage can pay the bills on time, pay themselves on time and have reduced or eliminated debts incurred to start the business. At last, these entrepreneurs feel on more stable ground and are freed from some of the stress and strain associated with early-stage cash-flow crunches. These entrepreneurs have begun to feel that they have "made it."

This is a critical time. At this stage, the entrepreneur, who has been struggling so long to make it, may feel tempted to start diverting resources into cars, houses, other business opportunities, or other things that have been sacrificed while the business was being developed. As the entrepreneurs' successes start to become more visible, they are often asked or pressured to become involved in very worthwhile industry or community projects. However, this is the most crucial time to stay focused and to avoid prematurely diverting money and/or time to other business, industry, community or leisure temptations. By staying focused, the entrepreneur builds cash reserves and strengthens the business to the point of real success.

What, exactly, is "real success?" The definition varies for every entrepreneur and may be measured in a variety of ways, such as those described in the remainder of this subsection.

### Industry Comparisons

The sales and profits levels that are considered "successful" for a business vary widely, depending upon the type of business. Success in one business might mean one hundred million dollars per year in sales, while in another business success may be achieved with only two or three million dollars per year in sales. When you are evaluating your success level, make sure you understand your business and value it in terms of your industry. How do your sales, profits, and return on investment compare with other similarly situated companies in your industry?

### Cash Reserves

The fact that a company is meeting its monthly operating expenses does not necessarily mean the company is a success. To be successful, a company should have cash reserves sufficient to cover at least three to five months of operating expenses. The cash reserves do not have to be all hard cash. They may be a combination of cash and lines of credit. The important goal is to have enough cash to cover your expenses when your sales are down so that you do not have to lay people off or change your lifestyle or the lifestyle of your employees.

### Sales Base

In conjunction with assessing your cash reserves, you must also consider the nature and condition of your sales base. Do you have a backlog of business, long-term contracts, or strong enough customer relationships so that your business is not just "hand-to-mouth?" A successful business has a sales base that it can count on month-in and month-out to generate sufficient income to cover ongoing operating expenses, plus maintain the cash reserves described above.

## *Profits*

One of the most common measures of the success of a business is the profit level of the business. People who want a quick assessment of your success will ask how profitable your business is. The profit level that is considered successful varies, depending on the industry. In some industries, profits equal to ten percent of sales after taxes may be considered successful. In other industries, success may mean generating profits equal to only two percent of sales.

Saying that a business should be profitable may seem painfully obvious. Often, however, when entrepreneurs see their sales taking off, they may begin to wheel and deal so much to continue bringing in the sales that they forget to think about profits. Losing track of profits is particularly easy to do if the entrepreneur isn't preparing and reviewing monthly financial statements. If the cash starts pouring in from sales and you are factoring or having a banker lending against your receivables, it may look like you've got sufficient cash and everything may seem wonderful. But beware! Before you jump to the conclusion that you have made it, make sure you have some accurate financial statements so you can determine if your profits are keeping up with your sales.

Maybe you think you are keeping accurate financials because you have a bookkeeper or internal accountant. Even if their numbers show you are operating at a profit, make sure that it is real profit. Be audited by an outside independent public accountant to determine if you do, in fact, have real profits. Too often, an internal accountant or bookkeeper forgets to take into consideration such items as returns and allowances, bad debts, obsolete inventory and some of the other legal or accounting requirements affecting the computation of profits. It is particularly important to have an outside professional review your books if you are about to raise money, apply for a loan, or sell your business. You don't want any big surprises, such as finding out you are really operating at a loss instead of a profit.

Making sure that profits are keeping up with sales doesn't mean that the entrepreneur should always avoid sales with low profits. Sometimes it may even be a brilliant sales move to go after sales with little or no profit in order to achieve good cash flow. You should always be thinking "profit" over the long term. However, if you are sitting on a lot of inventory and you need cash, it is understandable that you would want to convert that inventory into cash. You may decide to sell everything at your manufacturing cost or wholesale-acquisition cost so that you can turn that inventory into immediate cash for current expenses and new, more profitable inventory.

## Response of Financiers

Another measure of the success of a business is the response from banks and other financiers when the business is trying to borrow money, sell equity, or refinance.

Sometimes, companies that appear profitable and successful may find that banks are reluctant to make loans to them. The reason may be that, although business is going well, the company has reached a critical growth-phase. Banks and other financial institutions may evaluate the company and say to themselves, "Well, they made it through the start-up phase. They are starting to succeed in business and are approaching the phase where they are going to try to go from being an entrepreneurial business to being a real business. This is a critical juncture and we should wait to see how they come through it."

They know that you have reached the phase where you will start to change personnel and implement better systems in your company so that you have better financial reporting. You are transforming from an unstable "hope we make it" business to a viable, successful business. These are difficult times for a business no matter how successful it is, so financial institutions get nervous at this point. They are happy for you, but they also know that these are the times when the biggest mistakes are made. The entrepreneur might hire the wrong people or might make other mistakes that will cause the business to fail to reach the next level of stability and success. Once you make it to the next level, you will generally find it's easier to obtain money. Then a new, more professional growth pattern ensues.

When trying to determine if your success is real or imagined, keep in mind the different tiers or levels of growth that companies go through. Make sure you are "over the hump" of these various levels and not just moving up the hill. It's not always easy to tell. The indicators of success at one level may be different from those at the next level. For example, a debt-to-equity ratio of 8 to 1 may have been acceptable to the bank when you were making $300,000 a month in sales and requesting line of credit of $400,000. However, you may be shocked to find that, despite your apparent success when you are making $500,000 a month, the bank will not lend more money unless your debt-to-equity ratio is 5 to 1 or better. The potential loss is greater, so the bank becomes more conservative.

You may not be able to determine, yourself, whether or not you have made it over the hump to a new phase. The easiest way to find out is from the response of your potential financial sources. You are out there asking them for more money because your business is growing. When they are saying "no, no, no," not moving fast enough, or not giving you the valuation or terms you are seeking, then you know you haven't made it. Once they are willing to give you as much as you want, under the price and terms you want, then you know you are over the hump.

If you are trying to raise equity and have not made it over the hump, you will often find that you are having difficulty getting the price you want. You will also find that prospective investors are requiring all sorts of conditions before they will invest. For example, they may require that you hire more experienced staff for various management positions, strengthen your sales force, or acquire a new computer system. The real message they are giving you is that you're about to hit another growth curve. Until you get over the hump of that growth curve they're not going to give you the money you want on the terms you want.

All the input from investors may not be 100% correct, but they are generally giving you some good advice. They have looked at a lot more companies than you have. Even if you say "no" to their proposal, take their input seriously. Don't say, "Well, they're wrong, I'm going to go do it my way." They are in the business of evaluating and investing in companies, and their input may be just the advice you need to take you to the level of true success.

It can be very frustrating when your existing financial sources appear to be impeding your growth because of their reticence to more aggressively finance the business. Just remember that they are in the business of making money and want to invest in the best opportunities available. Rather than get frustrated and angry, which is easy to do, realize that you may not have sold them sufficiently on why your business is one of the best opportunities available. Take the time to deliver a well-planned presentation to the decision-makers of your investor source. Bring them up-to-date on the company's growth, future, improved systems and controls, and new management. You may be surprised at their lack of awareness of how your business has grown and changed. You may also be pleased with their responsiveness after you have sold them on why additional funding makes sense.

### *Business-Plan Goals*

Another measure of real success is the degree to which you've achieved the goals that you laid out for yourself in your business plan, assuming those goals would be considered benchmarks of success according to some of the other measures we have described. If your business-plan goals do not meet up to those other standards of success, then you should consider revising your goals.

### *Entrepreneur's Goals*

The entrepreneur's own personal goals may or may not be considered measures of success in the traditional business sense. Sometimes, the entrepreneur's goals may even conflict with the attainment of some of the other measures of success. For example, the entrepreneur may want to generate enough personal income to buy an elegant home, fancy car, yachts, country club memberships and other toys. He or she may want to have plenty of leisure time to spend with family and friends and the money to do so comfortably. Often an entrepreneur's goal is to build the business, sell it, and retire.

The attainment of such goals is certainly possible and desirable. However, their attainment may either cause the downfall of the business or may flow naturally as a result of the success of the business, all depending upon timing. The entrepreneur must strive to keep his or her personal goals in line with the goals for the success of the business, so that both are achieved.

## Strengthen the Core Business

❖ **The key to achieving real success is to develop and maintain a strong core business and to avoid the premature diversion of cash and time away from the business.**

The key to achieving real success is to develop and maintain a strong core business and to avoid the premature diversion of cash and time away from the business. The entrepreneur must constantly ensure that personal and business opportunities that arise from time to time are not allowed to weaken or slow the growth of the existing business.

This sounds very simple, but in reality can be extremely difficult. As success comes, so do opportunities. Now that you have a little extra cash, it is very easy to jump at these opportunities and later realize that they require more cash than you originally thought. Suddenly your core business begins to suffer as your cash and time are diverted. Make sure you have several month's cash reserves for your core business before financing new opportunities.

Before you can protect your core business, you have to understand exactly what that core is. The core business fills a specific market niche and generates a reliable and steady level of sales and profits. Sometimes you will hear the core referred to as the "bread and butter" of the business. It is the part of the business that the entrepreneur counts on day-in and day-out for a steady sales stream.

An example of a core business may be seen in accounting firms. Accounting firms have traditionally provided auditing services as a core business. As accounting companies grew, they began to diversify, adding management consulting and tax-return preparation to the services they offered. However, they always protected their core business and diversified as a means of growth, but always on a secondary level.

Sometimes you may think you know what your core business is. Then the definition of the core changes because the industry has changed. For example, in the early days of personal computers, a company might have classified its core business as being a software distributor. Then as the industry expanded and companies became more specialized, that same company might define its core business according to the type of software it distributed: business, education, entertainment, etc. Companies in this growing personal-computer industry began to focus on developing a strong foothold in their particular niche before diversifying to offer other software, peripheral or hardware products. Similarly, they more narrowly defined their customer base, dividing the market into retail resellers, corporate resellers, government resellers, mail order, mass merchants, etc. This allowed them to better understand the needs of each niche in order to more effectively serve their target market as the marketplace became more competitive. As the nature of the industry changes, you may need to modify the definition of your core business and customer base accordingly.

## Potential Temptations

❖   To succeed in the long run, keep your money and time focused on the business, even after it is succeeding.

❖   When diversifying, be sure your timing is right and try to select areas that will enhance the long-term profitability of your core business, with a minimum of risk.

❖   You can enjoy better and longer indulgence in your temptations if both you and your business are ready.

The entrepreneurs who succeed in the long run are generally the ones who keep their money and time focused on their business, even after the business is succeeding. Entrepreneurs who divert cash and time to other interests too soon after beginning to succeed can suddenly find themselves in a cash squeeze, unable to take advantage of sales and growth opportunities.

It is very tempting for the long-struggling entrepreneur to say "I've been working too hard. I just
have to take some money out of my company now
and enjoy life a little more. You only live once."
Ironically, the business owner who waits a little
longer and makes the business more stable by keeping time and money focused on it usually receives
greater financial reward and more personal freedom
sooner than the business owner who chooses to take
time and money out of the business each month before it reaches a point of real success.

The reason this is true is that the cash flow of
the growing business is generally controlled by the
banks and investors. The higher the profits, the more
valuable the business is in the eyes of those financing
sources. The entrepreneur can achieve higher profits
by not taking out too much cash for personal use and
not using cash too soon for business diversification.
Entrepreneurs who have made more for the investors and protected the bank's loans by personally
sacrificing or exercising restraint are in a stronger position when they want to raise more money, sell the
business, or do an initial public offering. These situations are where entrepreneurs obtain their BIG financial rewards.

The temptations for diverting time and money
come in many forms, some related to the business,
some to the industry or community, and others to
the entrepreneur's personal desires. Typical mistakes
include increasing personal or business overhead too
soon by acquiring "perks" (country club memberships, fancy cars, boats, etc.) or increasing salaries and
benefits that not only raise monthly cash requirements, but divert time away from the business. Another common mistake is trying to diversify the
business too quickly. Yet another temptation comes

from pressure on the entrepreneur to devote time and/or money to important industry or community activities. The temptation to contribute to what is clearly a good cause can sometimes divert the attention and resources of entrepreneurs before they and their businesses are really prepared. If the business is managed properly, the time will come when the entrepreneur can afford to give in to such temptations. The key is to be patient and wait until the right time.

Successful entrepreneurs spend their cash and time for purposes other than the business only when the time is right. First they build healthy cash reserves for the business and hire and train others to assume important responsibilities. This can be a frustrating time for business owners, who often "hate" to spend money on overhead for things they can do themselves. A philosophy of doing everything oneself can be okay for the entrepreneur who wants nothing more in life but to spend time on the business, just the way it is. However, for the entrepreneur who wants to further expand the business or spend more time and money on leisure or family activities, it is necessary to first invest in more people and opportunities for the core business. For every hour more you take off, you must have somebody covering for you. You must build a team of qualified people. To do so requires money, which means reinvesting some of your profits back into the business or having a profitable enough business to attract additional investment capital or loans.

## Business Diversification

There is nothing wrong with diversifying. In fact, diversification is a necessary step for generating business growth. The keys to successful diversification are to be sure your timing is right and to choose areas that will enhance the long-term profitability of your core business. Ideally, diversification will be in an area that relates to your core business, making it less risky. If the diversification is closely related to your current business, you may be able to use many of your existing assets (people and equipment), thereby reducing the initial cash requirements of your new venture.

Diverting time and cash from your core business before it is sufficiently strong can cause the core business to collapse. Generally, you will want to start diversifying only when you have sufficient cash reserves to sustain your core business for several months. This means that you should have enough money not only to pay the basic bills, like salaries and rent, but also enough money to buy the capital equipment and fund the marketing and advertising that are needed for your core business. Don't trick yourself into thinking you have sufficient cash reserves when you really don't.

When you diversify, you are basically starting another business. It almost always takes more cash and time than the entrepreneur first budgeted. Maybe your core business is doing well. Finally, for the first time, it is adequately capitalized. You think that now is the time to launch a new company to develop and market that new product line you've been thinking about. You put some money into the development of the new line. Then, suddenly, the product development is taking a little bit longer than you thought. There are some glitches. More and more of your time and money are being pulled into the new business. You find yourself saying, "Well I'll delay buying this for my core business.... I won't hire that new salesperson.... Oh, let's delay that marketing campaign a little longer because if I don't put money in the new business line, it's going to die." Pretty soon your core business can start to erode. All of a sudden the value of your stock starts declining and you are forced to divert money back from your new business to save your core business. Now you have two struggling businesses. Just when you thought you had achieved success with your core business, you find that real success is more out of reach than ever.

Do not divert funds from your core or primary business until you really have a solid cash reserve to fall back on. An adequate cash reserve should be several months of operating expenses plus an allocation for any personnel or capital equipment needed in the next several months.

When the time is right financially to diversify, the best way to do so is in areas related to your core business. That way, you will simply be building a broader base for your product or service, rather than starting a completely new business.

For example, assume you have a real estate development company. You are succeeding and you want to branch out. Your core business is the redevelopment of low-income housing. In low-income areas you refurbish apartments that have the potential for rapid appreciation because of rezoning, new businesses going into the area, or for some other reason. You know your particular geographic area very well and have made a lot of money in your niche. As you achieve success, it's very tempting to branch out into other real estate areas. Opportunities start presenting themselves everywhere. More realtors hear about you. Your phone is constantly ringing with news of more and more opportunities, many of them in different geographic areas and many involving real estate other than low-income housing. It's very easy to start looking at all these different opportunities and to stray from your niche. Pretty soon you are spread so thin that you are not devoting enough time to your core business. You start missing the opportunities related to that core. You're no longer able to follow up on your core leads on the spur of the moment, making sure to close the best deals before anyone else finds out about them.

Your best way to diversify may be to stay in the business of low-income housing, but simply move into another geographic area that is close to where you are currently developing. That way, you will take the same basic tools that you know very well and just apply them in a new market. That would make a lot more sense than developing beach-front properties at the same time or constructing new apartments in a new area. Even though the numbers might look great for these new types of developments, you would be getting yourself into very different fields. To really succeed in these new fields would be like starting over. Too many entrepreneurs find themselves immediately ready to leave behind what has made money for them and go, instead, for businesses with more glamor and ego-gratification. Stay with what has worked, diversifying only in related areas – at least until you have achieved real success. Then if you want to branch off into completely new areas, you can sell the successful business or hire other people to run it and devote all your time and energies to the new one.

## Outside Temptations

The entrepreneur who begins to succeed is confronted with temptations outside of the business, as

well as business opportunities. Outside temptations
lurk in such forms as:

- Family
- Toys – boats, cars, houses
- Country Clubs
- Charities
- Fame

As you can see from the list, it can be difficult to
detect or argue with some of the temptations. More
than likely, at least a part of the fuel for your energy
to start a business was an intense desire to indulge in
some or all of these temptations. The key to respon-
sibly dealing with temptations is to set goals and priorities and to understand where you are in terms of
accomplishing them. Remember, you can enjoy better and longer indulgence in your temptations if both
you and your business are ready.

Giving the cash and time demands of the business first priority for a period of time does not mean
that you value the business more. How can you say
that the business is more valuable than family, relax-
ation, or charities? You just have to realize that to
achieve the financial success and personal freedom
you desire in the long run, you may need to make
short-term sacrifices. If you ever reach the point that
the sacrifices seem too severe, then it may be time to
re-evaluate your goals. For example, maybe your goal
of achieving a net worth of ten million dollars before
spending more time with the family should be revised to three million dollars so it can occur sooner
with only minimal sacrifice in life-style.

If your business has drawn nearer to but has not
quite achieved real success, you might consider increasing your salary or taking a bonus to relieve per-

sonal financial stress. However, avoid taking money that will materially alter your life-style or excessively raise fixed costs for the business.

You don't have to postpone your toys and perks forever, only long enough so that enjoying them does not threaten the success of your business. Be sure that what you thought was real success doesn't turn out to be only imagined success. Otherwise, you may end up beginning the struggle all over again. It's hard enough to build a business once. To have to do it twice is even more difficult, particularly from a psychological standpoint.

As you become successful more and more people in the industry will want you to become a spokesman for the industry. Media representatives will want your time for interviews. A certain amount of speaking and media attention is good because it promotes your company, your products and your services. Nevertheless, you can reach the point of diminishing returns, where too many speaking engagements take too much time away from the business. As long as you are in charge of your business, your primary responsibility is to make payroll every month or every week and to grow your business so it will be there day-in and day-out. The business owners who keep their attention on the business are the ones who continue to enjoy its success year after year.

## The Big Reward

❖ **The entrepreneur will typically achieve greater financial success and greater personal freedom much sooner than his counterpart who is working for someone else.**

❖   YOU created the success, so YOU call the shots.
     YOU decide how and when to reward yourself.

All this talk of detours, hazards and pitfalls is
not meant to discourage you or to lead you to believe
that the entrepreneur is forced to work hard and sacrifice forever without a break. In fact, the entrepreneur will typically achieve greater financial success
and greater personal freedom much sooner than his
counterpart who is working for someone else.
It is possible to achieve whatever big rewards
you are seeking – time and money to spend on your
heart's desires; the fulfillment of having created a
successful business from a mere idea; fame; perhaps
even an early, financially comfortable retirement.
You just have to carefully and realistically plan your
road to success. You must also exercise patience and
restraint until you reach your destination. Don't get
impatient and look for shortcuts that aren't there.
Most businesses take at least four or five years, at
a minimum, to achieve real success. Four or five
years may seem like a long time to postpone the toys,
perks and other rewards. Keep in mind, however,
that most people who do not own their own businesses and who work for other people work at least
that long or longer before they begin to see promotions, benefits, and company perks. Furthermore, you
are your own boss and have the invaluable benefit of
creating and owning your own successful company,
unlike your corporate counterparts.
If it only takes five years to build a successful
business, just think how many times in your career
you can start from scratch and do it over again, if you
want to. Or you can take an early retirement and enjoy the temptations you postponed while you were
building the business. The options are limitless. You

created the success, so **you** call the shots. **You** decide
how and when to reward yourself.

## *Summary Tour*

### IMAGINED VERSUS REAL SUCCESS

* One of the most common detours for the entrepreneur is to mistake imagined success for real
  success.
* Measures of success include:

  * Industry comparisons
  * Cash reserves
  * Sales base
  * Profit levels
  * Response of financiers
  * Achievement of business-plan goals

### STRENGTHEN THE CORE BUSINESS

* The key to achieving real success is to develop
  and maintain a strong core business and to
  avoid the premature diversion of cash and time
  away from the business.

### POTENTIAL TEMPTATIONS

* To succeed in the long run, keep your money
  and time focused on the business, even after it is
  succeeding.

- When diversifying, be sure your timing is right and try to select areas that will enhance the long-term profitability of your core business, with a minimum of risk.

- You can enjoy better and longer indulgence in your temptations if both you and your business are ready.

## THE BIG REWARD

- The entrepreneur will typically achieve greater financial success and greater personal freedom much sooner than his counterpart who is working for someone else.

- **You** created the success, so **you** call the shots. **You** decide how and when to reward yourself.

# Chapter 10

# Conclusion

Before we bid you *bon voyage*, we have a few parting words. The authors' goal in writing this book has been to impart the following messages:

*To the Aspiring Entrepreneur* – Now that you have negotiated your way through the literary road map of entrepreneurship, we hope you have found your own entrepreneurial drive and are ready to explore the real-world entrepreneur's road map. Although this book has not provided <u>all</u> the answers to <u>all</u> the questions you will have along the way, we have tried to fuel the inspiration to travel and to provide the road and map by which to start your journey.

*To the Experienced Entrepreneur* – The authors know, from firsthand experience, that the entrepreneur's road can be lonely, especially in the start-up phase. We have designed this book so that you, the experienced traveler, may use it as a desk-top advisor and quick reference to help you through the many decisions and challenges that you face each day. When the road seems the toughest, it is often time to pull back from the confusion and go back to the basics. Our goal has been to help you do that.

*To the Intrapreneur* – If you have decided that starting a business is not appropriate for you at this time, we encourage you to explore the alternative route of becoming an intrapreneur. There is no reason why you shouldn't experience at least some of the rewards of the entrepreneur.

*To All* –

The authors' basic message has been to convey the reality that being an entrepreneur is a very natural thing to do. Should you succeed, the personal and financial rewards can be tremendous. The successful entrepreneur possesses a level of independence, freedom, accomplishment and self-esteem that others can only envy. The additional benefit of financial reward, which can range anywhere from a comfortable living to tremendous wealth, provides a sense of accomplishment and control over your own destiny.

We have not implied that the road is always easy or successful. In fact, there are many obstacles and sacrifices associated with being an entrepreneur, especially in the beginning. Not all businesses succeed. Nevertheless, whether you succeed or fail, it is best to know that you at least tried. The lessons learned in failure build character and prove invaluable for future journeys.

Often, one of the greatest obstacles to entrepreneurial success is getting started. The fear of failure and economic hardship, family responsibility, advice from those who do not understand, and fear of the unknown are all major culprits in preventing people from ever pursuing their dreams of starting a business.

This book has tried to overcome those fears. It has also attempted to point out other avenues, such as the concept of "intrapreneurship," where one can compromise a little by operating under the financial backing of a major company. More and more companies are beginning to work with employees to provide an environment that encourages employees to develop their entrepreneurial ideas within the company rather than leaving and forming new, potentially competing businesses.

The authors simply encourage people to get started in any way they feel comfortable – part-time, intrapreneurship, with partners or alone. Once started, all the fears begin to fade. Then, whether you succeed or fail, you will forever be a different, more aware, self-confident person.

The authors can speak firsthand of success and failure, having experienced both. They will readily admit that success is better. However, failure should leave you no worse off than if you never tried, provided you anticipate the risks and limit them from the outset.

For example, it is important to limit the amount of financial risk that you assume. You may have heard stories of how someone "bet everything" on the business. This is fine if you have nothing or very little to lose. However, if you have assets prior to your entrepreneurial venture, decide in advance how much you are willing to personally risk and stick to your plan. Do not be afraid to stress this point with potential investors and lending institutions.

This book has attempted to provide sufficient insight to common entrepreneurial issues and problems so that they can be anticipated, overcome, and/or avoided. In parting, there are three important concepts that we wish to emphasize.

First, expect that your business will change, especially as it progresses from the entrepreneurial

262 The Entrepreneur's Road Map

stage to more mature operational phases. In the beginning, a business usually cannot afford to have many of the administrative, legal and accounting controls common in larger companies. An inherent risk of a start-up venture is that it must often initially operate without many of these controls. The entrepreneur is forced to set priorities for allocating money, time and other resources. As the business begins to grow, however, the successful entrepreneur begins to "professionalize" the business as quickly as financially possible. Important systems and controls are added which will enable the business to move into a more stable, less risk-oriented phase.

Realizing that businesses change as they grow, successful entrepreneurs constantly look ahead to anticipate those changes. They plan and budget for new people, buildings and equipment; invest in financial control systems; research new sales and/or product opportunities; and continually update their business plans.

The second concept we wish to re-emphasize is a warning – don't celebrate your success too soon. As we pointed out earlier, when a business appears to be on the verge of success, one of the most common reasons for failure is that the entrepreneur too quickly diverts time and money to things other than running the core business. The most common errors are diverting time and money to leisure, industry or community activities and/or attempting overly aggressive and unplanned diversification or expansion.

Lastly, always remember that the environment and goals the entrepreneur creates and sets for the company are vital. Common complaints heard in growing companies are that "We are losing our entrepreneurial spirit;" or "Things have changed – that old sense of teamwork is gone." Inevitably, companies must change as they grow; however, it is important throughout the changing times to maintain an environment that breeds success rather than bureaucracy and false security. Oftentimes, as entrepreneurs find themselves further and further from the day-to-day activities of their businesses, they become frustrated and isolated. During this evolutionary growth phase, it is imperative that the entrepreneur continually create the environment and set the goals that will enable the company to smoothly make the transition from an entrepreneurial to a professional company.

In summary, becoming a successful entrepreneur is a natural thing to do and is, in fact, done with surprising regularity. The rewards are within your grasp. So what are you waiting for?

*Happy Traveling!*

# Appendix A

# The Entrepreneur's Business Start-up Checklist

Once you have selected a business concept or product, there are a number of steps that need to be taken to create the business and protect your idea. For your convenience, we have prepared a checklist of things to do to start your new business.

The checklist highlights many basic requirements to consider in starting your business. We have not attempted to list the many detailed steps that the entrepreneur must take to complete these tasks, research ideas and develop strategies. We have, however, tried to provide sources, leads and helpful hints for completing each step. We have also included estimated time and money required to accomplish many of the tasks. (Of course, costs will differ depending upon geographic area and changing rates.) Not every business will need to take every step listed in this checklist. Also, the order in which the steps should be taken will not be the same for every business. Nevertheless, the checklist should at least point you in the right direction as you begin your entrepreneurial journey.

There are many sources of additional advice and assistance for the entrepreneur, many of which are available at no cost or low cost. Often local Chambers of Commerce distribute checklists of local government requirements for starting a business, as well as telephone numbers and addresses of government offices to contact for further information. The Small Business Administration provides courses and distributes literature concerning most every step for starting a business. Colleges and universities often offer courses for entrepreneurs, and some even sponsor "incubators" for start-up businesses. For compliance with legal and government regulations, the government offices responsible for administering the regulations and monitoring compliance will furnish information and answer questions. Most local and state governments have general information numbers to call for direction to the proper office for handling your questions. Most telephone directories also provide extensive government-office listings. If you have questions about industry-specific regulations or issues, you may find trade associations that can provide helpful information. In Appendix C, we have compiled a list of resources that may help you in your search for answers to particular types of questions.

A few telephone calls should lead to all the information and resources you need for most any area where you need assistance. You may run into a few "dead ends." You may also occasionally become frustrated with getting busy signals, being placed on hold and being referred back and forth between offices and departments. If you are persistent, however, you should be able to find the answers and guidance you need.

This checklist is not meant to provide legal or accounting advice. Although you can accomplish many of the tasks on your own, there are some tasks

where the wisest thing to do is seek (
sional advice. The more you learn (
however, the more effectively and eco1
can use the services of the professionals ,

## *Establishing the Company*

_____ **Business Plan**
See the chapter on "Planning Your Itinerary"
and Appendix B, "Sample Outline of a Business
Plan."

_____ **Name Availability**
You are not legally required to check into the
availability of a name you are considering for your
company or product. This is, however, a very important step to take. If you do not take this step you
might choose a name that is confusingly similar to a
name that someone else is using for a similar purpose. This could expose you to liability for trademark
infringement. You might then be forced to change
the name you have selected and/or pay damages to
the party whose name you have infringed. Before
you choose the exact name for your business or
product, there are steps you can take to assure yourself that the name you are considering is not confusingly similar to a name already being used or reserved for use by someone else. Places to check to see
if a name is already in use or reserved for use include: the corporation, trademark and fictitious name
registry offices of states where you will be operating;
the United States Patent and Trademark Office
(where federal trademarks are registered); telephone
directories of cities where you will be doing business;
and trade name directories. If you prefer to pay
someone else to perform the search for you, you can

contact a trademark attorney or a trademark search firm, such as Thomson and Thomson, whose telephone number is (617) 479-1600. Having someone else perform the search for you may cost around $250 to $600, depending upon how many resources are consulted and how fast you need the information. If you have any doubt about whether your proposed names are similar enough to someone else's names to be in danger of infringement, you should consult a trademark attorney. The advice could save you from many hassles and expenses down the road. Once you have selected a name and assured yourself that it is available, there are steps you can take to protect the name from being used by someone else. The name for a corporation may be reserved by filing a form with the state where you will be incorporating and paying a nominal fee. This step will need to be taken only if you plan to incorporate but will have some delay before your articles of incorporation are filed with the state. The reservation will remain valid for a short period of time, usually 30-90 days, depending upon the state. Once you have incorporated, the name will become a part of the state's public record for as long as your corporation remains in good standing. To fully protect names chosen for your products or services, you should register with federal and state trademark offices. For guidance on how to do this, see the section on "Trademarks" discussed later in this Checklist.

### Logo and Slogan Selection

If you are going to use a logo or slogans in connection with your business or product, you will need to exercise the same precautions that you did in selecting your name. You will need to be careful not to infringe someone else's logo or slogan. As you are searching trademark records for names already in use, you should also search for registered logos and slogans that are similar to the ones you are considering. You should also seriously consider registering your logo and slogans with the United States Patent and Trademark Office.

_____  **Form Your Business Entity**
When deciding which form of business entity to choose for your company, you will have a variety of options to consider. Some of these options include a sole proprietorship, a partnership and a corporation. There are also specialized forms of these entities, such as a general partnership, limited partnership and an "S" corporation. Each type of entity carries its own special tax, liability, and other legal and accounting characteristics. We recommend that you learn as much as possible about the options on your own. Most bookstores and libraries carry books written for the non-expert that discuss these entities in detail. Also, the Small Business Administration and many local colleges offer courses and distribute brochures or outlines designed to help the business owner decide which form of business entity to choose. Once you understand the basics, then you can hire an attorney experienced in advising businesses to answer any unresolved questions and prepare the necessary legal documents. Assuming you have done some background research on your own and assuming your proposed business structure is not unusually complicated, the cost of forming a corporation or partnership may run around $350 to $1,500. If your company is going to be a sole proprietorship, you may incur no costs other than the costs of your research because no legal documents are required to form a sole proprietorship. Forming a partnership or

corporation may take around two to four weeks on the average. Do not rush the process. Make sure you thoroughly understand your options before reaching a final decision. It is possible to start out as one form, such as a sole proprietorship, and later convert to another form, such as a corporation, but you should understand the implications of doing so. The laws concerning the formation of a partnership or corporation vary from state to state. You will need to be sure that you have complied with applicable state laws in forming your entity.

_____ **Fictitious Name Registration**
        Many, but not all, states require a business operating under a "fictitious name" to register that name (usually with the court clerk of the county where the business is located). If you are a sole proprietorship, a fictitious name would be any name other than your own. If you are a corporation or partnership, a fictitious name would be any name other than the legal name of your company. For example, if ABC, Inc. does business under the name "Al's Electric," the name "Al's Electric" would be a fictitious name. Some states not only require registration of a fictitious name but also require that the name be published in a selected newspaper to see if anyone objects to its use. The exact requirements for fictitious name registration are governed by state law. Guidance for obtaining the forms and complying with the registration procedures may be obtained by contacting your state corporation office, your county court clerk, or your attorney. The fees for fictitious name registration are usually minimal – $20 or less. If newspaper publication is required, that may cost another $25-$50. This process may take several weeks. Many banks require evidence you have completed

the process before they will allow you to open a bank account in the name of your business.

_____ **Letterhead and Business Cards**
Letterhead and business cards often create the first visual image of a company. They lend credibility to the existence of a company, no matter how small or informal it is. You can expect to invest several hundred dollars on this purchase. Ordering letterhead and business cards can force certain other decisions, such as what to do about a location, telephone number and fax machine. If you have not made a decision about the location, you could start out with a post office box address. As for the telephone (and fax machine, if you can afford it), if you do not yet have an office, consider installing a separate telephone line for the business in your home.

_____ **Federal Tax Employer I.D. Number**
All businesses are required to have a Federal Tax Employer Identification Number assigned by the Internal Revenue Service. Contact the nearest IRS office for the necessary forms to apply for the number. There is no charge associated with obtaining the number. This number will be needed for filing tax returns and will also be requested information on almost all credit applications.

_____ **Open Checking Account**
This can be an exciting step in the creation of a new business. The exact requirements for opening an account will vary from bank to bank. Most require a copy of your articles of incorporation (if your company is a corporation), a copy of your fictitious name registration (if one was required), your Federal Tax I.D. Number, a resolution from your board of direc-

tors authorizing the opening of the account, and signature cards for the people who will be signatories on the account. The dollar amount of deposit required may vary from as little as $100 to several thousand dollars, depending upon the type of account and its privileges.

_____ **Business License**
You will need a license to do business in the city or town where your business is located. Contact your local City Hall for instructions on how to apply for a business license. The initial license may cost as little as $25 or as much as several hundred dollars. In most cases, a business license must be renewed annually. A renewal fee or local business tax is usually imposed each year and is usually based on a percent of income from the operation of your business. In addition to a local business license, some types of businesses (such as real estate and construction companies, attorneys and health care professionals) must obtain special state licenses prior to beginning business. Contact your state's business licensing office to find out if a state license is required for your business.

_____ **Locate Initial Financing:**
See the chapter on "Financing the Expedition."

_____ **Establish accounting system**
The earlier you establish and begin maintaining an accounting system for your business, the fewer headaches you will have at tax time, the more prepared you will be to meet with investors and lenders, and the more effectively you will be able to manage the business. Trying to reconstruct financial transactions months after-the-fact requires much more time

and effort than taking a few minutes each day to record those transactions in a systematic way. If your business uses a computer, you will find a variety of accounting software programs (costing anywhere from around $100 to several hundred dollars) available. Many of those programs have even been custom-designed for specific industries. An accountant may also assist with setting up your books.

_____   **Payroll**
If all goes well, the entrepreneur will finally get to the point of issuing paychecks to employees. The success of this moment may sometimes be clouded by the onslaught of additional paperwork. Income, social security and unemployment tax withholding requirements (see "Payroll-Tax Withholding Requirements" discussed later in this Checklist), workers' compensation insurance and other payroll-related issues often seem like an impossible maze. The penalties for failure to comply with these requirements are severe, so it is extremely important to be sure you comply from the time you begin issuing payroll checks. You can contact federal, state and local taxing authorities (the numbers are in your telephone book) for payroll-tax compliance instructions. Your state government information office can direct you to the proper source for information on workers' compensation insurance. We strongly advise contracting with a payroll service at the earliest possible point to help ensure compliance with all applicable laws. Payroll services are in the business of cutting payroll checks and preparing all of the withholding checks and forms required by government authorities. The charge for such a service varies based on the number of employees, the number of times per month you issue checks and the way the checks are

delivered to you (by courier, mail, or some other method). Often payroll services charge a minimum processing fee based on paying around ten employees. However, payroll services may still be cost-effective if you have even fewer employees. A business with ten employees might pay around $40-$100 per month for checks issued twice a month. Usually, the more employees you have, the less you are charged per check prepared by the payroll service. If you have fifty or more employees, you may be paying only $.50 or less per check. In most instances, the fees charged by a payroll service are a small price to pay for having someone else handle the paperwork headaches.

### Insurance

There are many types of insurance available for the entrepreneur. Some are clearly more important in the early stages of the business than others. One of the first types of insurance a company needs to purchase is liability insurance to protect against losses or damages suffered by other people under circumstances where the business might be held liable. If the company markets a tangible product, product liability insurance should be purchased right away to protect the entrepreneur from being devastated by lawsuits associated with the product. Liability insurance coverage in excess of $1,000,000 is not uncommon for a business. One of the most common types of insurance coverage carried by businesses is property insurance protecting against damage to property caused by fire, vandalism, theft, windstorms and other casualties. The amount and types of insurance that should be carried by a company will depend upon the type of business being operated; the risks associated with the operation of the business; legal requirements applicable to such business (such as workers' compensation insurance requirements); medical and other insurance benefits provided to employees; and, in some cases, the requirements of agreements with third parties. For example, leases often specify minimum property insurance requirements. A professionally-qualified insurance agent, broker or consultant may assist with an analysis of risks and potential liabilities and may recommend a plan for the amounts and types of coverage. Insurance coverage should be re-evaluated periodically as a business grows and changes. The costs of insurance coverage vary dramatically depending upon the carrier, the type of policy, the risks covered and policy exclusions. It pays to shop around for the rates and coverage most appropriate for your specific situation.

_____ **Occupancy and Building Permits**
You will need to check with the government information office of the city or county where your business will be located to find out what permits, if any, you might need. Many local governments require that companies obtain an occupancy permit to occupy a particular office or retail space for a particular purpose. If you plan to perform any construction or alteration of your office or retail space, a building permit will probably be required.

_____ **Sales and Use Tax**
See the section on "Sales and Use Tax" discussed later in this Checklist.

_____ **Resale Tax Number**
See the section on "Resale Tax Number" discussed later in this Checklist.

### _____ UPC Symbol

If your company plans to market a product that will be sold through supermarkets or other stores that sell mass-market merchandise, you will need to obtain a Universal Product Code ("UPC") number to include on the wrapper or cover of the product. The UPC number is the code composed of lines and bars that is scanned by computerized cash registers at the check-out counter. The UPC number is not legally required, but some stores will not carry a product unless it has a UPC number on it. The UPC number is assigned by the Uniform Product Code Council, Inc. located at 8163 Old Yankee Road, Suite J, Dayton, Ohio 45458, telephone number (513) 435-3870. The cost is around $300 for a small company and up to several thousand dollars for a larger company, plus $50 to $200 for the art work needed to make the symbol. It takes two to ten days to have the UPC number assigned, depending upon the form of delivery, plus two to three days for the art work. Some industries, such as the book-publishing industry, use scanning codes in addition to or instead of the UPC. You should check with other companies in your line of business or trade associations for your industry to find out the standard for your industry.

### _____ Import/Export Licenses

If your business entails importing and/or exporting goods from or to foreign countries, then various licenses may be required. Information may be obtained from a number of sources, including customs brokers, import/export consultants, or the appropriate offices within the United States Department of Customs.

_____ **Agreements**

Almost all new businesses require certain contractual agreements. Some examples include confidentiality or non-disclosure agreements, employment agreements, sales rep agreements, stock option agreements, credit applications, distribution agreements, consulting agreements and lease agreements. We recommend collecting some of these agreements in advance of when you think you might need them. Doing so can be helpful for two reasons. First, you will develop an understanding of contractual issues before you encounter a situation where such an understanding is called for. Second, having agreements already prepared may put you in a position of basing an agreement on your form (which, of course, contains your preferred terms) rather than someone else's form (which will be drafted from their point of view). Stationery stores often sell sample contracts for various situations. Also, there are many books that contain sample agreements. Many trade associations have compiled and published suggested forms of agreements for their industries. We are not encouraging you to play lawyer for yourself. Rather, we are suggesting that you educate yourself in the basics and use your attorney economically and prudently.

## Taxes

_____ **Payroll-Tax Withholding Requirements**

If your company pays salaries to one or more employees, whether part-time or full-time, it must comply with federal and state requirements concerning payroll-tax withholding and payment. For example, an employer must withhold federal taxes from employees' paychecks and periodically deposit these funds with the Internal Revenue Service. Furthermore, the employer must deduct social security payments from each employee's check and must match with corporate funds the total deducted from all checks. These social security funds must also be deposited periodically with the federal government. In addition to federal tax requirements, most states also require the employer to withhold and pay to the state amounts for state income tax and unemployment insurance. All of the necessary forms and instructions can be obtained from the Internal Revenue Service and the tax authorities in states where you will be doing business. As suggested earlier in this Checklist under "Payroll," a payroll service may be very helpful in complying with tax withholding and filing requirements.

_____ **Sales and Use Tax**
Companies that sell products to end users are responsible for charging and collecting sales tax, and then paying such taxes to the appropriate state tax authority. Companies that do not sell to end users, but rather sell to resellers, such as manufacturers and distributors, are generally exempt from charging and collecting such taxes. Many states exempt certain classes of merchandise or customers from the sales and use tax requirements. Companies qualifying for such exemptions should set up their records to account for exempt sales to avoid over-paying taxes. All companies are subject to a sales and use tax audit by the government. Therefore, it is important to comply and keep accurate records. If your company is subject to sales tax, you must file sales tax reporting forms for each required reporting period, even during periods when you have not made any sales. Information on these taxes may be obtained from state taxing authorities.

_____ **Resale Tax Number**

Companies purchasing goods to be resold, such as retail stores, should obtain a resale tax number. This number allows the holder to purchase goods without paying tax at the time of purchase. For information on obtaining this number, contact your state tax office. In some states, the sales tax number and the resale tax number are the same.

_____ **Income Tax Requirements**

Each company must pay quarterly taxes on its income. Depending upon the type of entity you have chosen, these payments will be made by the entity, itself, or by the owners (in the case of sole proprietorships, S Corporations and partnerships). These periodic income tax payments are required by the federal government and most states. Also, many local jurisdictions impose taxes on the income of businesses operating within their boundaries. Your accountant, payroll service or federal, state and local tax offices should be able to assist you with determining the requirements and procedures for such taxes. One little reminder – you must file income tax returns for each required reporting period, even if your company did not make any money or lost money.

_____ **Property Tax Requirements**

State and local governments may impose taxes on real and personal property owned by the company. Information on these taxes may be obtained from state or local taxing authorities.

_____ **Business Transfer Tax Requirements**

Some states impose taxes upon the termination or transfer of a business. In some states, the purchaser of the business is required to withhold from the purchase price an amount sufficient to cover the transfer tax. Also some states provide that the failure to withhold such amount may subject the purchaser to personal liability for the payment of taxes, interest and penalties owed by the former owner with respect to the business. If you are buying or selling a business, you should look into these requirements.

## Corporate Formalities

**If you operate your business as a corporation, there are certain formalities that you will need to observe in order to maintain the corporation in good standing and to ensure that the stockholders and directors will enjoy the full benefits of protection from personal liability. These include:**

### Corporate Organizational Documents

To form a corporation, you must file articles of incorporation with the state in which you wish to incorporate. Your corporation will need to hold an organizational meeting, documented by minutes, for such purposes as approving the formation of the corporation, issuing stock, electing officers and directors and adopting bylaws. Most states will provide forms for incorporating. It is also possible to buy "packaged" bylaws and minutes. The contents of all of these documents are extremely important because they determine the rights and obligations of the corporation and each of its stockholders, officers, and directors. Therefore, it is advisable to seek the advice and assistance of an attorney experienced in corporate law when forming your corporation. That will help ensure that the company is established in accordance with the desires of its founders and the laws of the applicable state. If you wish to be an "S" Corporation, an additional form must be filed with the Internal Revenue Service by a certain deadline to qualify for the "S" Corporation tax benefits for a particular year. Your local IRS office will provide the appropriate form and filing instructions.

_____ **Qualification to do Business**
If your corporation will be engaged in business in any states other than the state in which your corporation was formed, you may need to qualify to do business and maintain a registered agent in such states. Your attorney may provide guidance as to whether or not the degree of business conducted would require qualification and, if so, the procedures for becoming qualified.

_____ **Stockholders' Agreement**
A corporation is not required to have a stockholders' agreement. Nevertheless, if your company has more than one stockholder, you should seriously consider having a stockholders' agreement prepared and signed. A stockholders' agreement determines rights and obligations of the stockholders and the corporation concerning issues such as the following: disposition of the stock of stockholders who wish to withdraw from the business and/or transfer their stock; disposition of the stock of a deceased or disabled stockholder; covenants-not-to-compete with the corporation; protection of trade secrets and intellectual property; etc. It is important to enter into such an agreement at the earliest possible time. Going through the process of negotiating the agreement often helps the parties clarify what they expect of each other and of the business relationship. It is much easier to resolve such questions at the beginning of

the relationship when the stockholders are coopera-
tive, rather than at a later time when the stockholders may have had a dispute that has lead one or more
of them to want to sever the working relationship.
The stockholders' agreement is important for establishing control and other rights of the stockholders.
The provisions needed in such an agreement may
vary significantly from one corporation to another.
Therefore, you should consider seeking the advice of
an attorney experienced in drafting stockholders'
agreements when you are ready for one.

### Annual Report

Each state requires the filing of an annual report for corporations formed or qualified to do business in such state and the payment of an annual fee
(and, in many states, an annual franchise tax). Failure
to file such report and pay such fee(s) may result in
the dissolution of a corporation or the loss of its qualification to do business. Forms for filing annual reports are usually mailed by a state to the registered office of a corporation one or two months before the filing deadline. It is very important that you file this
form each year in order to maintain your corporation
in good standing. Find out from your attorney or
state corporation commission the filing date for the
annual report in your state of incorporation. If you
do not receive the necessary annual report form at
least thirty days before the filing date each year, you
should contact the state corporation commission to
request that a form be mailed to you.

### Annual Meeting

Each year the stockholders and directors of the
corporation must hold an annual meeting for the
election of officers and directors and the transaction

of other business concerning the corporation. The procedures for holding this meeting are specified in the corporate bylaws. Minutes of the annual meeting should be kept in the corporate minute book. In most states, the stockholders and directors may sign minutes unanimously consenting to actions rather than actually holding formal meetings to approve such actions. If you need assistance in complying with the requirements for the annual meeting, you should contact your attorney at least 60 days prior to the scheduled date for such meeting.

_____ **Regular or Special Meetings**
From time to time, you may wish to hold regular or special meetings of your corporation to approve the ongoing activities of the company. It is advisable to hold such meetings to approve major activities of the corporation, such as the execution of important contracts, borrowing money, expanding the business, etc., and to keep minutes of such meetings in your minute book. The purpose of holding meetings to approve such actions is to ensure that they will be considered duly approved actions of the corporation and not actions of the individual directors and officers. Otherwise, the officers and directors may become personally liable for the actions taken. When calling and holding such meetings, you should do so in accordance with the procedures outlined in your bylaws. As pointed out above, in most states, unanimous written approval of minutes and actions taken is an acceptable alternative to actually holding meetings, but you should confirm that this is true in your state.

_____ **Indemnification**
A major advantage of the corporate form of operation is that it usually protects stockholders from personal liability for actions taken by the corporation. The bylaws or articles of incorporation should indemnify the stockholders, directors and officers of the corporation to the greatest extent permitted by law for actions in their corporate capacities, other than intentional or grossly negligent misconduct. From time to time, a state may amend its corporate laws to permit expanded indemnification. You should consider having your corporate documents reviewed by legal counsel every year or two to be sure they provide the maximum allowable indemnification protection.

## Partnership Formalities

Usually, fewer formalities are required to form and operate partnerships than corporations. The following points, however, should be kept in mind:

_____ **Partnership Agreements**
There are two types of partnerships – (1) a **general partnership,** in which each of the partners is personally liable for the obligations of the partnership and (2) a **limited partnership,** consisting of at least one general partner and one limited partner. In a limited partnership, the general partner(s) is (are) fully liable for the partnership's obligations and control the partnership's business. The limited partners have limited liability and rights of control. There is no requirement that a general partnership have any sort of written agreement to be legally considered a partnership. Nevertheless, for their own protection, the partners should enter a partnership agreement

that spells out their respective rights and obligations. There are a number of formalities required for the formation and operation of a limited partnership. If you are considering either of these forms of doing business, you should consult with an attorney concerning the potential liabilities and the agreements needed.

_____ **State Filings**

Although far fewer formalities are required to form and operate partnerships than are required for corporations, some states require the filing of a partnership certificate for general partnerships. Also, most states require the filing of a partnership certificate for a limited partnership, as well as the observance of certain other formalities. Furthermore, as pointed out earlier in this Checklist, sometimes a partnership must file a fictitious name registration (see "Fictitious Name Registration"). You can contact your state government for information regarding filings required for partnerships.

## *Protection of Intellectual Property*

Intellectual property, such as trademarks, patents, copyrights and trade secrets may constitute very valuable assets of a company. They may provide the company's advantage over its competitors, generate goodwill and marketing power, and be a principal force behind the company's success. The protection of intellectual property should be considered early in the formation of the business. Failure to take adequate steps to protect such property at the outset may lead to complex and expensive legal actions later on and may cause you to forfeit the right to prohibit others from using your company's creations. You can take some protective measures on your own. Others, such as patent applications, are best handled through attorneys who specialize in the protection of intellectual property.

_____ **Trademark Protection**
Earlier in this Checklist, we talked about the reasons why it is important to be sure you are not infringing someone else's trademark (see "Name Availability" and "Logo and Slogan Selection"). We also suggested that you take steps as soon as possible to protect names, logos and slogans you have selected. We strongly suggest filing federal trademark or service mark registrations for your business and product names, logos and slogans. These are filed with the United States Patent and Trademark Office in Washington, D.C. The trademark office will send forms and applications. The number to call is (202) 557-3158. The current filing fee is $175 per application (a separate application is filed for each mark). You might also consider filing state trademark applications in the states where you will be doing business. State registrations are often approved faster than federal registrations and may provide better notice to others in your state that your names are not available for use by others. If, for financial reasons, you must choose between a federal and a state registration, you should apply for federal registration. It provides much broader protection.

_____ **Copyright Protection**
Copyright protection is available to the authors of "original works of authorship," including literary, dramatic, musical, artistic and certain other intellectual works (such as computer programs). For works created after March 1, 1989, a copyright notice

is not required to protect the work from copyright infringement. To obtain the fullest protection under copyright laws, however, it is best to include a copyright notice and register with the federal Copyright Office. The copyright notice consists of the word "Copyright," the abbreviation "Copr." or the symbol ©, together with the name of the copyright owner and the year of first publication. Some attorneys advise using both the word "Copyright" and the © because using both may afford wider international protection. The addition of the phrase "All Rights Reserved" is also advisable because such phrase is required for copyright protection by the laws of some foreign countries. You may register copyrighted material with the Copyright Office of the Library of Congress. Such registration is required if you have need to enforce your rights in federal court. Timely compliance with registration regulations may also entitle you to certain additional rights, such as the award of statutory damages and attorneys fees against infringers. The filing fee is $10 and the registration is effective on the date the Copyright Office receives all of the required elements of the application. For further information, you may contact the Copyright Office at (202) 479-0700. If you use employees or consultants to help you develop copyrightable materials for your company, be sure to have a written agreement in advance specifying that your company will own the copyright.

_____ **Patent Protection**
    If your business involves the creation of an invention, you should first determine if the invention violates the patent rights of anyone else. You should then seriously consider trying to obtain a patent registration for your invention to protect it

from unauthorized use or infringement by others. The patent process is a very technical and complicated process. It is possible to research and apply for a patent for your invention on your own. If you can possibly afford it, however, you should have an attorney who specializes in patent law prepare your application. Subtle variations in the wording of an application may greatly increase or diminish the protection afforded by your patent. The cost for preparing a patent application varies, depending on the invention and the attorney. It could easily cost several thousand dollars. If you are uncertain about incurring this expense, you might consider at least spending an hour or two with an experienced patent attorney to discuss the pros and cons of proceeding with your application.

### Trade Secrets

A trade secret is a formula, discovery, methodology, process, device or combination of information that is not generally known and that gives a company an advantage over competitors who do not know or use it. If a company does not take adequate protective precautions, its trade secrets may lose their classification as trade secrets. The company may then lose its power to prevent others from using these valuable resources. One important step for protecting trade secrets is to require employees, consultants and others who have access to your trade secrets to sign confidentiality and non-disclosure agreements.

# *Financing/Expansion*

\_\_\_\_\_ **Securities Disclosure and Registration**

When raising money to fund the start-up or expansion of a business, there are detailed federal and state disclosure and registration requirements that must be met, unless the business qualifies for an exemption or exclusion from such requirements. Failure to comply may result in substantial civil and criminal penalties for the company, its owners, officers, directors and agents. An attorney who specializes in this area should be consulted as to the applicability of such requirements to any fund-raising efforts planned by your business before you solicit or accept any funds from a third party.

\_\_\_\_\_ **Business Expansion**

If you wish to expand your business to multiple locations and you wish to involve other people and/or their capital in that expansion, there are numerous alternatives and factors to consider. You may expand through franchise, distributorship or licensing arrangements; additional company-owned units; joint ventures; or a variety of other options. Each option is subject to complicated legal and financial requirements and restrictions, particularly if your expansion is considered a "franchise" or "business opportunity" under applicable state and federal laws. The advice of an attorney or business consultant who is experienced in these areas should greatly facilitate the decision-making process and help avoid legal pitfalls.

## Other Operational Considerations

#### _____ Pension and Profit-Sharing Plans and Other Fringe Benefits

Businesses may set up a pension and profit-sharing plan and other fringe benefits for employees. In some cases these plans and benefits may result in tax deductions for the business and may be treated as non-taxable or tax-exempt for the employee. Generally, corporations are entitled to more tax benefits in connection with the offering of fringe benefits than are other forms of business organizations. The rules and regulations concerning such plans and fringe benefits are extremely complex, so you should consult with an accountant, attorney, or other investment advisor who is experienced in this area to ensure that such benefits are structured and administered properly to meet tax requirements.

#### _____ Employee-Related Laws and Regulations

There are a wide range of laws and regulations related to employees. For example, the Immigration Reform and Control Act of 1986 requires employers to maintain specific records on each employee verifying that such employee is not an illegal alien. Failure to meet these requirements may subject the employer to civil and criminal penalties. There are also a variety of federal and state laws concerning such employee-related issues as workers' compensation insurance, discrimination, minimum wages, health and safety requirements, and labor relations. Many of these employee-related laws apply to both small and large businesses. Government agencies regulating these areas may be contacted for information concerning compliance requirements.

_____   **Consumer-Protection Laws**

There are a number of state and federal laws designed to provide protection to consumers, such as laws regulating product warranties, consumer credit, product advertising, the sale of business opportunities, and product labeling. A business should investigate the application of such consumer-protection laws to each new type of product or service that it offers. Trade associations often provide their members with useful information on such topics. Also, there are many helpful books and articles that discuss the basics of complying with consumer protections laws.

_____   **Anti-Trust Laws**

Federal and state anti-trust laws govern such areas as illegal price fixing; refusals to deal with a competitor, supplier or customer; charging different prices to different customers; certain territorial restraints; attempts to create monopolies; and other areas that restrain competition and interfere with the operation of the free market. Although often thought to apply only to large businesses, certain anti-competitive practices may subject even a small business to liability under these laws. Product manufacturers and distributors, in particular, need to seek legal counsel experienced in these issues.

_____   **Industry-Specific Laws**

Sometimes laws are enacted that regulate the licensing and operation of specific industries and businesses. For example, there are a number of laws applicable to real estate, construction, banking and other financial-related businesses. Trade associations and government regulatory offices, as well as attorneys, may provide guidance regarding the existence and compliance with such laws.

_____ **International Laws**

If your business imports or exports products or otherwise engages in business abroad, there are a wide variety of laws and regulations that should be investigated. We have already referred to licensing requirements earlier in this Checklist (see "Import/Export Licenses"). You may learn a lot about applicable international laws by consulting with appropriate government offices and embassies. It is also advisable to consult with an attorney having an expertise in the laws of the countries with which you will be dealing.

_____ **Mail-Order Sales**

In response to problems with late or undelivered mail-order merchandise, the Federal Trade Commission ("FTC") issued a Mail Order Rule. The rule requires shipment of merchandise by the date specified by the seller (30 days, if no date has been specified). If orders are not shipped on time, the seller is required to notify customers and provide an opportunity to cancel the order or receive a refund. The FTC will send you information on this rule if you call (202) 326-3768. You should also check with your state government to find out if your state imposes additional regulations on mail-order sales.

_____ **Telemarketing and Door-to-Door Sales**

If telephone or door-to-door sales are part of your planned sales strategy, you should check the laws of the states where you will be selling. Many states have enacted laws that regulate the manner in which such sales may be conducted.

# *Appendix B*

## *Sample Outline of a Business Plan*

**COVER PAGE**: List the name, address and telephone number of the business and the names and titles of the principals of the company.

**STATEMENT OF PURPOSE**: State the purpose of the plan. If you are using the business plan to raise money, state how much, what form (debt or equity), and the proposed use of the proceeds.

**TABLE OF CONTENTS**: Provide a detailed table of contents, similar to the format of this outline. This will facilitate the reader's easy reference to specific parts of the plan. We recommend the use of tabs to identify the major sections of the plan.

I.   **SUMMARY**: In three pages or less, give a summary overview of the business. Include the products or services offered, the location, the target market, what distinguishes your business from competitors' businesses, the key management staff, financial highlights, projected development schedule, and statements of why you believe your business will be (continue to be) successful.

## II. THE BUSINESS

A. DESCRIPTION – A brief description of the products or services of the business, location, experience, goals and philosophies, why the business will be (is) successful.

B. MARKET – Niche, size, characteristics, growth, customers, need.

C. COMPETITION – Names and descriptions of primary competitors; what distinguishes your business from theirs.

D. SALES AND MARKETING PLAN – Sales force, methods of sales and distribution, advertising and promotion, evolution of product line, price, seasonality, market penetration, growth strategy.

E. MANAGEMENT AND KEY PERSONNEL – Names, titles, past experience and accomplishments.

F. MILESTONE SCHEDULE – Schedule for accomplishing milestones for the development of the business.

## III. FINANCIAL DATA

A. INTRODUCTION

    1. Planning and Control Objectives
    2. Organization & Personnel; Auditors
    3. Use of Proceeds and Investor Liquidity

B. HISTORICAL FINANCIAL DATA (Existing businesses only)

    1. Income Statement and Balance Sheets for Prior Three Years (Audited Statements, if applicable)

2. Tax Returns

## C. INCOME PROJECTIONS

1. Summary
2. Detail by Month for Year 1
3. Detail by Quarter for Years 2 & 3 and Annually for Years 4 & 5
4. Notes and Assumptions

## D. CASH-FLOW PROJECTIONS

1. Summary
2. Detail by Month for Year 1
3. Detail by Quarter for Years 2 & 3
4. Notes and Assumptions

## E. CURRENT BALANCE SHEET

## F. EQUIPMENT AND FACILITIES – Description, cost, lease, buy, when, depreciation.

## G. PERSONNEL AND COMPENSATION – Hiring schedule, cost, ratios (e.g. sales per employee), important compensation plans and fringe benefits.

## H. FINANCIAL ANALYSIS

1. Source and Application of Funds
2. Key Ratios and Statistics – Debt to equity, return on investment, current ratio, sales per employee, inventory turnover, break-even point.
3. Additional Financings

**IV. SUPPORTING DOCUMENTS**: Documents that provide more detail than is necessary for the main body of the business plan, but which are useful as supporting information, may be presented in an appendix or separate volume. Such documents might include credit reports, key contracts, leases, letters of intent from prospective customers, resumes, job descriptions, flow charts, etc.

# Appendix C

## Resources

Throughout the book, we have suggested some specific resources that you might approach for additional information and assistance on specific topics. For quick reference, we have compiled a list of those resources. We have also added some others that were not discussed in the text. We recommend exploring your local library, bookstores and Small Business Administration Office for these and other helpful resources. Also, check with colleges and universities in your area. Many of them offer special programs, courses, libraries and assistance for the entrepreneur and "incubators" for new businesses.

### BOOKS

Alarid, William and Berle, Gustav. *Free Help from Uncle Sam to Start Your Own Business (or Expand the One You Have).* Puma Publishing, 1988.

Davidow, William H. *Marketing High Technology: An Insider's View.* Free Press, 1986.

Fucini, Joseph J. and Fucini, Suzy. *Entrepreneurs: The Men and Women behind Famous Brand Names and How They Made It.* G.K Hall & Co., 1985.

Godin, Seth and Conley, Chip. *Business Rules of Thumb.* Warner Books, 1987.

Hoge, Cecil C., Sr. *Mail Order Moonlighting.* Ten Speed Press, 1976.

Hopkins, Tom. *How to Master the Art of Selling.* 2d ed. Warner Books, 1980.

J.K. Lasser Tax Institute. *How to Run a Small Business.* Bernard Greisman, editor. 5th ed. McGraw-Hill, 1982.

Liles, Patrick R. *New Business Ventures and the Entrepreneur.* Richard D. Irwin, 1974.

MacKay, Linda Howarth. *Financial Management: How to Make a Go of Your Business.* Small Business Management Series No. 44. U.S. Small Business Administration, 1986.

McCormack, Mark H. *What They Don't Teach You at Harvard Business School.* Bantam Books, 1988.

Osgood, William R. *Planning and Financing Your Business: A Complete Working Guide.* Inc./CBI Publications, 1983.

Resnik, Paul. *The Small Business Bible: The Make-or-Break Factors for Survival and Success.* John Wiley & Sons, 1988.

Riles, Al and Trout, Jack. *Marketing Warfare.* McGraw-Hill, 1985. Reprint. First Plume Printing, 1986.

Riles, Al and Trout, Jack. *Positioning – The Battle for Your Mind.* McGraw-Hill, 1981. Revised. Warner Books, 1986.

Stanton, William J. *Fundamentals of Marketing.* 3d Edition. McGraw-Hill, 1971.

Waymon, Lynne. *Starting and Managing a Business from Your Home.* Office of Business Development Starting and Managing Series, Volume 102. U.S. Small Business Administration, 1986.

White, Richard M., Jr. *The Entrepreneur's Manual: Business Start-ups, Spin-offs, and Innovative Management.* Chilton Book Company, 1977.

## FEDERAL GOVERNMENT AGENCIES

We recommend that you check your local telephone book to see if there are local offices of the following agencies in your area:

**Anti-Trust Laws**
Federal Trade Commission
(202) 326-2222

**Business Information, General**
Small Business Administration
(202) 653-6600
Small Business Answer Desk
(800)368-5855

**Consumer Product Safety Information**
Consumer Product Safety
Commission
(800) 638-2772

**Copyright Information**
Copyright Office, Library of
Congress
(202) 479-0700
(202) 707-9100 For forms

**Employment Issues**
Equal Employment Opportunity Commission
(202) 663-4264
Department of Labor
(202) 523-7316
Federal Labor Relations
Authority
(202) 382-0748

**Franchise Regulation**
Federal Trade Commission
(202) 326-3128

**Import/Export Information**
U.S. Customs Service
(202) 566-8195

**Mail-Order Sales Regulation**
Federal Trade Commission
(202) 326-3768

**Patent Information**
Patent and Trademark Office
(202) 557-3158

**Securities Law and Filing Information**
Securities and Exchange
Commission
(202) 272-7450

**Social Security Information**
Social Security Administration
(Check local listings)

**Statistics: Business and Census**
Department of Commerce
(202) 377-2000

**Trademark Information**
Patent and Trademark Office
(202) 557-3158

**Tax Information (Federal)**
Internal Revenue Service
(202) 488-3100
(Be sure to also check
local listings

## FINANCIAL INFORMATION

The following resources list detailed information concerning specific companies and financial institutions. These resources are multi-volume publications carried by most of the larger public libraries.

*Dun & Bradstreet Reference Book.* Six times a year. Dun & Bradstreet Credit Services, Dun & Bradstreet, Inc., One Diamond Hill Road, Murray Hill, N.J. 07974. Contains the names and financial ratings of businesses of all types located throughout the United States and Canada. Dun & Bradstreet also publishes other specialized reference books and directories.

*Moody's Bank and Finance Manual.* Annual with twice-weekly supplements. Moody's Investors Service, 99 Church Street, New York, N.Y. 10007. Indexes American banks and financial institutions, listing their officers, directors, and other top-level personnel, as well as financial information.

*Standard & Poor's Security Dealers of North America.* Semi-annual. Standard & Poor's/McGraw Hill, 25 Broadway, New York, N.Y. 10004. Lists brokers, dealers, underwriters, securities distributors, and investment banking firms of the United States and Canada. Details names of officers and key personnel, addresses, telephone numbers, and specialization.

## MAGAZINES

There are many business magazines. The following are two whose focus is the start-up or growing business. We recommend looking over these and other magazines at your public library or newsstand to see if they are of interest to you.

*Entrepreneur*
    For Subscription Info:    1-800-421-2300
                                 1-800-352-7449 (Calif.)

*Inc.*
    For Subscription Info:    1-800-234-0999

## MANUFACTURERS

*Thomas Register of American Manufacturers.* Annual. Thomas Publishing Company, One Penn Plaza, New York, N.Y. 10001. Lists manufacturers, producers, and similar sources of supply in all lines.

## STATE AND LOCAL GOVERNMENT INFORMATION

Most state and local governments have a general information telephone listing. This is the best place to start if you do not know exactly which office you need to contact.

## TRADE ASSOCIATIONS

Trade associations can be a source of invaluable information concerning specific industries. The following are two directories of names, addresses, telephone numbers and membership characteristics of trade associations. Most public libraries carry one or both.

*Encyclopedia of Associations.* Bienniel. Gale Research Company, Book Tower, Detroit, Mich. 48226.

*National Trade and Professional Associations of the United States & Canada and Labor Unions.* Annual. Columbia Books, 1350 New York Ave, N.W., Suite 207, Washington, D.C. 20005.

## TRADE NAMES

The following is one of the places to check to see if anyone is already using a name that you are considering for your company or product. It is also helpful for locating competitors and possible resources for your business. Many public libraries carry this publication.

*Trade Names Dictionary.* Donna Wood, editor. 7th ed. Gale Research Company, Book Tower, Detroit, Mich. 48226. Identifies trade names for consumer products and their manufacturers, importers and distributors.

# Glossary of
# Financial Terms

*The following are definitions of many of the financial terms used throughout the book. Also included are terms which were not discussed but which you will probably encounter in your dealings with financial institutions and investors.*

ACCOUNTS PAYABLE – Money owed by a company to its business creditors from whom it has bought goods or services on credit.

ACCOUNTS RECEIVABLE – Money that is owed to a company by its customers who have bought goods or services on credit.

ACCOUNTS RECEIVABLE FINANCING – Financing for a company that is obtained either by selling its accounts receivable (factoring) or by pledging the accounts receivable as security for the repayment of funds that have been borrowed. If a company borrows against its receivables, the receivables still appear on its balance sheet. On the other hand, if the receivables are sold to a factor, they disappear from the seller's balance sheet. Accounts receivable financing and factoring are the most common type of loans obtained by entrepreneurial companies. Lenders who provide these types of loans generally require the personal guaranty of the borrower. *See* FACTORING and GUARANTY.

**ASSETS** – The valuable property, resources and property rights owned by a business. Assets include such items as cash, inventory, real and personal property, equipment, and accounts receivable. They also may include intangibles of value, such as goodwill, franchise or license rights, patents and trademarks. On the balance sheet, assets are equal to the equity plus the liabilities of the company. *See* ACCOUNTS RECEIVABLE, BALANCE SHEET, EQUITY, INVENTORY and LIABILITIES.

**BALANCE SHEET** – The "financial picture" of a business at a particular point in time. The balance sheet lists the assets, liabilities and equity of the company on a specific day. On the balance sheet, the assets should always equal the liabilities plus the equity. *See* ASSETS, EQUITY and LIABILITIES.

**BOOK VALUE** – The value of an asset as shown on the books of account of the owner of the asset. The book value may be different from the market value. The book value of common stock is determined by dividing the net worth of the company (total assets minus total liabilities) by the number of shares of stock outstanding. *See* ASSETS, COMMON STOCK, LIABILITIES and NET WORTH.

**BONDS** – Certificates that contain written promises to pay the purchasers of the bonds a specified sum of money (the face value of the bond) at a fixed time in the future (the maturity date), with interest at a specified rate payable on designated interest dates. The sale of bonds is a form of debt financing. Bonds are often issued by public entities to fund special projects or to generate money to loan to businesses to encourage industrial development. *See* DEBT FINANCING.

**BREAK-EVEN POINT** – The actual or projected point in time when a business will neither incur a loss nor make a profit. At the break-even point, a company's income has reached the level to exactly cover all of the company's expenses. *See* PROFIT.

**BRIDGE LOAN** – A loan taken out for a short period of time to finance a business until other longer-term financing can be arranged.

**CASH FLOW** – The flow of cash into and out of a business. A cash-flow analysis helps predict when additional cash will be needed to meet a company's operating requirements.

**COLLATERALIZED LOAN** – A loan secured by a security interest in some named asset(s) (the "collateral") of the debtor. If the borrower defaults in repaying the loan, the lender has the right to apply toward repaying the loan the proceeds from whatever specific assets the borrower has pledged as security or collateral. A commercial lender may require a business to pledge its inventory, accounts receivable or other assets as collateral for a loan. *See* ASSETS, ACCOUNTS RECEIVABLE, INVENTORY and SECURITY.

**COMMON STOCK** – Certificates representing an ownership (equity) interest in a corporation. With only a few exceptions, all corporations issue common stock. The common stock generally entitles the stockholders to voting rights and rights to receive dividends. Many corporations issue only common stock. Other corporations may finance operations by issuing other forms of equity, such as preferred stock, various classes of common stock, or warrants. If preferred stock is issued, the holders of common stock are entitled to dividends only after the dividend rights of the preferred stockholders have been satisfied. Common stockholders, however, usually have greater voting rights than preferred stockholders. When a company is prospering, the common stockholders have an advantage over preferred stockholders. The common stockholders have an unlimited interest in the profits of the company, while the preferred stockholders receive dividends at a fixed rate. On the other hand, if a business is not doing well, the preferred stockholders are in a better position. They are guaranteed dividends at a specified rate, while the common stockholders share in what is left over. If a corporation dissolves, holders of common stock are entitled to receive only what is left after all other parties (including preferred stockholders) with superior claims have been satisfied. *See* DIVIDEND, EQUITY, PREFERRED STOCK and WARRANTS.

CONVERTIBLE DEBT – A form of debt (such as a promissory note or a bond) that gives the holder of the debt instrument the option to convert the debt into a common stock or other equity interest in the debtor company. Often the convertible debt carries a lower interest rate than debt without conversion privileges. The advantage to the holder of the debt is the possibility of participating in the increased value of the debtor's stock if the company prospers. *See* COMMON STOCK, DEBT and EQUITY.

CONVERTIBLE PREFERRED STOCK – A class of preferred stock that entitles the stockholders to convert their stock into some other form of security, usually a stipulated number of shares of common stock. Ordinarily, the conversion is at the option of the stockholder and must be exercised within a specified period of time. An owner of convertible preferred stock would typically exercise this right of conversion when, in the opinion of the stockholder, the dividend income, voting rights, or other privileges of the common stock are sufficiently enticing to more than offset the security surrendered by a change from preferred to common stock. *See* COMMON STOCK.

CURRENT ASSETS – Cash and other assets of a company that are expected to be converted to cash, sold or consumed within one year of the balance sheet date, the most common of which are accounts receivable and inventory. *See* ACCOUNTS RECEIVABLE, ASSETS, BALANCE SHEET and INVENTORY.

CURRENT LIABILITIES – All debts of a company that fall due within one year of the balance sheet date, the most common of which are accounts payable, accrued payroll, accrued taxes and short-term bank debt. *See* ACCOUNTS PAYABLE, BALANCE SHEET, DEBT, and LIABILITIES .

CURRENT RATIO – A measure of a company's ability to meet its financial obligations coming due during a business year. The current ratio is calculated by dividing the current assets by the current liabilities. Although there are exceptions, most lenders and investors like to see a current ratio of at least 2:1 (twice as many current assets as current liabilities). *See* CURRENT ASSETS and CURRENT LIABILITIES.

DEBT – Something owed by one party to another. In the business context, the debt is usually money which the business has borrowed from another party and which must be repaid.

DEBT FINANCING – Money that is borrowed to finance a business. Debt financing carries an obligation to repay the debt at a designated interest rate over a specified time period. Repayment may be in one lump sum or in installments (of principal and interest or interest, only) on designated dates. Examples of debt financing include secured loans, unsecured loans and bonds. *See* BONDS, SECURED LOAN and UNSECURED LOAN.

DEBT-TO-EQUITY RATIO – The ratio calculated by dividing a company's liabilities (accounts payable, taxes payable, salaries earned but not paid, bank debt, etc.) by its equity (retained earnings plus capital invested by owners). Most lenders and investors look at this ratio in determining whether or not to lend to or invest in a company. *See* DEBT, EQUITY, LIABILITIES and RETAINED EARNINGS.

DIVIDEND – A fund set aside from the profits of a corporation to be distributed to stockholders. Dividend also refers to the proportional amount of such fund that is distributed to the holder of each share of stock. *See* PROFIT.

EARNINGS – *See* PROFIT.

EQUITY – The ownership interest in a company. The extent to which a company's assets exceed its liabilities. *See* ASSETS and LIABILITIES.

EQUITY FINANCING – Money that is raised to finance a business by selling an ownership interest in the business. Some forms of equity sold to finance a company include common stock, preferred stock, and limited partnership interests. *See* EQUITY.

FACTORING – The sale or transfer of accounts receivable. Companies use factoring to obtain immediate cash rather than wait to collect amounts owed. The company acquiring the accounts receivable (the "factor") assumes the risk of collection. As compensation for assuming the risk and responsibility of collecting the accounts receivable, the factor acquires the accounts receivable at a discount. In other words, the seller of the receivables receives less than the full value of the receivables. The discount is usually equal to a stated percentage of the total receivables being transferred. In factoring, the receivables are generally sold without recourse. This means that the factor cannot turn to the seller if it is unable to collect balances owed. *See* ACCOUNTS RECEIVABLE.

GUARANTY – An undertaking by one party to be responsible for the payment of a debt or the performance of a duty of another if the party with the payment or performance obligation defaults. Lenders often require business owners to sign personal guarantees for money loaned to the business. Such personal guarantees would allow a lender to look to the personal assets of the business owner as a source of repayment in the event the business defaults in repaying a loan.

INITIAL PUBLIC OFFERING ("IPO") – A corporation's first offering of stock to the public. IPO's often provide the opportunity for existing investors to make big profits since, for the first time, their shares will be given a market value reflecting expectations for the company's future growth. *See* PUBLIC OFFERING.

INVENTORY – The value of a business's raw materials, work in progress, supplies used in operations, and finished goods purchased or made for resale and currently owned by the business. Oftentimes labor costs directly associated with manufacturing a product will also be valued as part of the inventory. The value of a company's inventory can vary with fluctuations in the cost of raw materials. Consequently, there are several acceptable methods of valuing inventory. The most common are First In, First Out ("FIFO") and Last In, First Out ("LIFO"). The term "inventory" is also used to refer to an itemized listing of all the components in inventory, including, at a minimum, the cost, part number, description and quantity. Sometimes lenders require that the inventory of a business be pledged as security for a loan. *See* SECURITY.

**INVESTMENT BANKER** – A firm that acts as an intermediary to bring together and structure deals between companies seeking financing and parties with funds to invest.

**LIABILITIES** – In the financial context, a company's debts. Liabilities include such items as accounts payable, notes payable, money owed for expenses which have been incurred but not paid, money owed for taxes, and amounts due bond-holders. *See* ACCOUNTS PAYABLE, BONDS, DEBT, and NOTES PAYABLE.

**LINE OF CREDIT** – A credit arrangement under which a financial institution agrees that it will lend money to a customer up to a specified limit. A line of credit is usually arranged before the funds are actually required. It provides flexibility for a business by ensuring the ability to meet short-term cash needs as they arise. Funds advanced under a line of credit may be unsecured, but lenders often require that advances be in the form of accounts receivable financing, inventory financing, some other form of secured loan or backed by a personal guaranty. *See* ACCOUNTS RECEIVABLE FINANCING, COLLATERALIZED LOAN, GUARANTY, INVENTORY and UNSECURED LOAN.

**MEZZANINE FINANCING**– In venture capital language, the stage of a company's development just before it goes public. Investors during this stage have a lower risk of loss than previous investors. They can look forward to early capital appreciation as a result of the market value gained during an initial public offering. *See* INITIAL PUBLIC OFFERING.

**NET WORTH** – The excess of a company's assets over its liabilities; also referred to as equity. *See* ASSETS, EQUITY and LIABILITIES.

**NOTES PAYABLE** – Money owed by a company to a bank or other lender.

**OPTION** – A form of investment where the option-holder has the right to buy (call) or sell (put) a specific security or commodity within a specified time at a fixed price. The price paid for an option is not refundable if the option is not exercised. If the option is exercised, the price of the option may be applied toward the purchase price. *See* SECURITY.

**PREFERRED STOCK** – A class of stock in a corporation that entitles its owners to certain preferences over the holders of common stock of the same corporation. Preferred stock usually has preferred rights to dividends (in a fixed amount or at a fixed rate) and a preferred position over common stockholders for the distribution of assets upon liquidation. Preferred stock usually does not have voting rights. *See* ASSETS, COMMON STOCK and DIVIDEND.

**PRICE/EARNINGS (P/E) RATIO** – A stock analysis statistic computed by dividing the current price of a stock by the current (or sometimes the projected) earnings per share of the corporation. A relatively high price-earnings ratio is usually an indication that investors believe the company's earnings are likely to grow. *See* EARNINGS.

PRIVATE PLACEMENT – A direct sale of securities to a limited number of investors to raise equity financing. Many companies choose to raise money through a private placement rather than a public offering because it is usually faster, less expensive, and subject to much fewer disclosure and reporting requirements. Private placements are subject to many restrictions on how and to whom they may be sold. Stock purchased through a private placement is also subject to restrictions on transfer. It is, therefore, less liquid than stock purchased through a public offering. *See* EQUITY FINANCING, PUBLIC OFFERING and SECURITY.

PROFIT – The excess of a company's income over its expenses (including taxes). Also referred to as "Earnings."

PUBLIC OFFERING – An offering to the investment public of new securities. Companies offering securities through a public offering must comply with complex disclosure, registration and reporting requirements of the Securities and Exchange Commission. *See* SECURITY.

RETAINED EARNINGS – The profit of a company over a specified period of time minus the dividends paid to stockholders over the same period. *See* DIVIDEND and PROFIT.

SECOND-ROUND FINANCING – An intermediate stage of venture capital financing. It comes after the early start-up or seed-money stage and before the mezzanine level. *See* MEZZANINE FINANCING, SEED CAPITAL and VENTURE CAPITAL.

SECURED LOAN – *See* COLLATERALIZED LOAN.

SECURITY – 1. INVESTMENT-RELATED: A document or certificate evidencing an ownership interest in a corporation (a stock certificate), a creditor relationship with a company or governmental entity (a bond) or the right to ownership in a company (an option or warrant). 2. FINANCE-RELATED: Collateral offered by a debtor to a creditor as security for a loan or other debt. *See* COLLATERALIZED LOAN.

SEED CAPITAL – The first round of financing for a new venture. Seed capital investors generally assume that the continuing costs of the business will be financed from some other source, such as operating income or later stage financing. Also called "Start-up Capital."

START-UP CAPITAL – *See* SEED CAPITAL.

UNSECURED LOAN – A loan that is not backed by security or collateral. *See* COLLATERALIZED LOAN.

VENTURE CAPITAL – A pool of risk capital, often contributed by large investors, which is used to finance young, small (often high-risk) companies that have good growth prospects but are short of funds. Venture capital investors are willing to assume the risk of investing in companies that meet their investment criteria in hopes of realizing a high rate of return on their investment as those companies grow. Sources of venture capital include but are not limited to wealthy individuals, subsidiaries of financial institutions (banks, insurance companies, etc.), and funds raised and/or managed by investment banking and stock brokerage firms.

**VENTURE CAPITALIST** – The party that manages a venture capital fund. *See* VENTURE CAPITAL.

**WARRANT** – A security that entitles its owner to purchase a specific number of shares of stock at a predetermined price within a specified time period. A warrant may be sold separately or in conjunction with a bond, short-term note, certificate of preferred stock or other security. *See* BONDS, PREFERRED STOCK and SECURITY.

**WORKING CAPITAL** – The difference between current assets and current liabilities. The cash available to meet the current expenses of a company. *See* CURRENT ASSETS and CURRENT LIABILITIES.

# Index

Accountants 148, 158, 176, 226, 229, 273, 279, 290
Accounting System 272-273
Accounts Payable 303
Accounts Receivable 75, 155, 175, 303
Accounts Receivable Financing 153, 155, 303
Acquiring a Business 58, 62-63
Action, Need for 28-29
Advertising 119-122
Advisors 225-235
Agreements 277
Alternatives to Creating a Business "From Scratch" 58-64
American Motors 105
Anti-Trust Laws 291, 298
Apple Computer 11, 106
Assets 304
Ashton-Tate 40-41
Attorneys 89, 129, 148, 158, 160, 173, 176, 226, 228, 231, 232, 233, 277, 280-291
Authors, Background 4-6, 41

Balance Sheet 304
Banks 80, 129, 137, 143, 146, 151-154, 155, 270, 271, 307, 311, 313
Baskin-Robbins Ice Cream 39
Beatles, The 106
Body Glove 103, 104
Bonds 141, 164, 304, 306, 308, 310, 313, 314
Books, Business 297-298
Book Value 169, 304
Break-Even Point 295, 305
Bridge Loan 305
Brokers 166, 176-177
Building Permits 275
Burger King 103
Business Advisors

Compensation 231-233
General 225-235
Selecting 225-229
Working With 230-233
Business Cards 271
Business Diversification 250-253
Business Entity, Forming 269-270
Business Expansion 289
Business Ideas
    Analyzing
        Expertise 52-53
        Financial Return 54-57
        Financing 50-52
        General 43-57
        Risk Comfort-Level 53-54
        Time Considerations 47-50
    Discovering 37-42
Business Judgment 205-206
Business License 272
Business Opportunity Laws 289
Business Partners 65-67
Business Plan
    General 71-86, 267
    Outline 293-296
    Preparation 77-84
    Presentation 84
    Purpose 71-77, 128, 130, 132, 134, 138, 142, 152, 157, 158, 169, 175, 176
    Resources 78
Business Transfer Tax 279-280

Calvin Klein 106
Cash Flow, Defined 305
Cash-Flow Problems
    Avoiding 74-77, 175-176
Chambers of Commerce 266
Checking Account 271-272
Checklist for Starting a Business 265-292

Choosing a Business (See Selecting a Business Idea)
Christian Dior 106
Cofounders 65-67
Collateralized Loan 305
Commerce, Department of 52, 78, 299
Commissions 159, 188, 197-199, 215-216
Common Stock 305-306
Communication 22-24, 207-208
Compaq Computer 11
Compensation 197-199, 215-216
Competition 95,294
Computerland 103, 104
Consistency 204, 206-207
Consultants 225-235
Consumer-Protection Laws 291, 299
Convertible Debt 306
Convertible Preferred Stock 306-307
Copyright Office of the Library of Congress 287, 299
Copyrights 285, 286-287
Core Business
    Defined 247
    Discussed 238
    Strengthening 246-248
Corporate Sponsors 146, 162-163
Corporation
    Annual Meeting 282-283
    Annual Report 282
    General 269-270, 280-284
    Indemnification 284
    Organizational Documents 280-281
    Qualification to do Business 281
    Regular Meetings 283
    Special Meetings 283
    Stockholders' Agreement 281-282
Creating the Image (See Image, Creating the)
Creativity 2, 6, 10, 16-18, 19, 26
Current Assets 307
Current Liabilities 307
Current Ratio 307
Customer
    Importance of 87-90
    Service 87, 100-101
Customer Financing 146, 164-165
Customs Service, 276, 299

dBASE 40, 104
Debt, Defined 307
Debt Financing 140-142, 146, 147, 149, 152, 164, 174, 307-308
Debt-to-Equity Ratio 152-153, 154, 308
Detours 237-258
Digital Equipment Corporation 103, 104
Direct Sales 187, 188, 190, 196, 198, 199
Discrimination 290
Distribution
    Channels
        Direct Sales 188
        Distributors 189
        Mail Order 187
        Retail 186-187
        Sales Representatives 188-189
        Selecting 186-195
        Telemarketing 187
        Using Effectively 195-199
        Wholesalers 189
    General 183-202
Distributors 189
Distributorships 60-61
Diversions 248-255
Dividend 308
Domino's Pizza 102
Door-to-Door Sales 292
DuPont 105

Earnings (See Profits)
Earn-Out 170-172
Edison, Thomas 18, 25
Egghead Software 106
Emerging Industries 40, 41
Employee-Related Laws 290, 299
Entrepreneur
    Alternatives to Creating a Business "From Scratch 58-64
    Defined 9

Entrepreneur (Continued)
 Traits
  Action 28-29
  Communication 22-24
  Creativity 16-18
  Flexible Planning 18-20
  General 9-31
  Optimism 20-21
  Persistence 26-28
  Realism 21-22
  Risk-Taking 24-26
  Self-Belief 11-15
  Simplicity 15-16
*Entrepreneur* Magazine 300
Equal Opportunity Commission 299
Equity, Defined 308
Equity Financing 140-142, 144, 146, 147, 149, 152, 153, 154, 155, 160, 163, 166, 167-171, 308
Experience, Value of 34-35, 52-53
Exxon 108

Factoring 146, 153, 155, 308-309
Federal Express 105
Federal Tax
 Employer Identification Number 46, 271
Federal Trade Commission 164, 299
Federated 108
Fictitious Name Registration 270-271
Financial Expectations 33, 35-36, 43, 72-73
Financial Information 300
Financial Projections 72, 74-77, 80-83
Financing 127-182, 289
 Ongoing Business 173-176
 Projections 295
 Sources 147-167
  Banks 151-154
  Corporate Sponsors 162-163
  Customer Financing 164-165
  Factoring 155
  Family and Friends 149-150
  Foreign Resources 165
  Franchising 161-162
  Government Sources 164

 Grants 165
 Investment Bankers 158-159
 Other Alternatives 166
 Personal Funds 148-149
 Private Investors 150-151
 Public Offering 159-161
 Venture Capital 155-158
 Strategies 127-145
 Structuring the Deal 167-173
 Timing 173-176
Financing a Business 50-52
Financing Phases 145-147
Financing Sources 147-167
Financing Strategies 127-145
 Amount of Financing 139-142
 Good Marketer 133-135
 Investor Relations 144-145
 Investor Selection 143-144
 Multiple Sources 129-131
 New Concepts 138-139
 Positive Attitude 135-138
 Presentation Hints 131-133
Finders 176-177
Flexibility, Importance of 18-20
Ford Motor Company 11, 105
Ford, Henry 11
Foreign Resources 165
Franchises 52, 60-61, 161-162, 289, 299
Fringe Benefits 290
Frye, Art 38

Geneen, Harold 77
General Motors 105
Government Sources of Financing 164
Grants 165
Grateful Dead, The 106
Guaranty 153, 309

Health and Safety Requirements 290

IBM 11, 90, 103, 104
Image, Creating the 91, 97-114
Imagined versus Real Success 237-246
Immigration Reform and Control Act of 1986 290

Import/Export Licenses 276
*Inc.* Magazine 5, 148, 300
Income Tax 279
Incubators 148, 266
Industry-Specific Laws 291
Initial Public Offering 145, 146, 309
Insurance 274-275
Insurance Agents 226, 274
Intellectual Property
    Protection of 285-288
Internal Revenue Service
    271, 277, 278, 281, 299
International Laws 292
Intrapreneur
    Defined 3-4
    Discussed 58, 63-64, 162, 260
Inventory 309-310
Inventory Turnover 75-76
Investment Bankers 146, 154, 158-
    159, 310
ITT 77

Keep it Simple 15-16, 212-213
Key Employees, Agreements with
    221-222

Labor, Department of 299
Laser Technology 26
Lawyers (See Attorneys)
Lead Time 47-50
Leadership 204-211
Leading by Example 210-211
Letterhead 271
Leveraging 141
Levi's Jeans 97
Liabilities, Defined 310
Licensing 53, 58-60
Line of Credit 153, 154, 310
Liquid Paper 38
Liz Claiborne 106
Loans, Secured 153, 313
Loans, Unsecured 153, 313
Location 113-114
Logos
    Importance 102-103
    Protecting 108-109, 268-269, 286
"Lotus 1-2-3" 104

Magazines, Business 300
Mail Order 44-57, 187, 299
Mail Order, Regulation 164-165, 292
Management
    Agreements with Key
        Employees 221-227
    Defined 204
    General 203-223
    Qualities 204-211
        Communication 207-208
        Consistency 206-207
        Leading by Example 210-211
        Respect for Others 208-209
        Self-Confidence 206
        Self-Understanding 211
        Sound Business Judgment
            205-206
        Teamwork 209-210
    Techniques
        General 211-220
        Keep It Simple 212-213
        Management by Exception
            214-215
        Management by Motivation
            215-216
        Management by Objective
            213-214
        Reviewing and Revising
            Goals 217
        Selecting Management
            Team 217-220
Management by Exception 214-215
Management by Motivation 215-216
Management by Objective 213-214
Management Team 217-220, 294
Management Team, Importance of
    73-74, 84
Manufacturers 44-57, 301
Market Niche 16, 34, 36, 41, 42, 92-97,
    294
Marketing
    Compared with Sales 183-185
    Creating the Image 97-114
    Defined 91
    General 87-126
    Philosophy and Strategy 87-92
    Pricing 114-119
    Promoting the Product 119-122

Marketing (Continued)
    Selecting the Target Market 92-97
Marketing Strategy, Defined 91
McDonald's Restaurants 90
Mezzanine Financing 145, 146, 310
Micropro 104
Microsoft 104
Microwave 38
Milestones 79-80, 140, 168, 171, 172, 176, 294
Minimum Wages 290
Mrs. Fields Cookies 39
Multiple of Earnings 168-173

Name
    Choosing 102-108, 267-268
    Protecting 108-109, 267-268, 286
Nesmith, Bette 38
Net Worth 311
Notes Payable 311
Nordstrom Department Store 90, 102

Occupancy Permits 275
Optimism 12, 20-21
Option, Defined 311

Partnership
    Agreements 284-285
    Discussed 269, 284-285
    Limited 269, 284, 285
    State Filings 285
Patent and Trademark Office, U.S. 267, 269, 286
Patents 285, 286, 287-288
Payroll
    General 273-274
    Service 274, 278
    Taxes 273, 277-278
Pension and Profit-Sharing Plans 290
Percy, Dr. 37
Persistence 26-28
Pet Rock 98
Planning, Importance of 18-20
Post-it Notes 38
Preferred Stock 141, 311
Price/Earnings Ratio 168-172, 311-312

Pricing 114-119
Private Placement 158, 312
Product Appearance 109-113
Product Value 99-102
Profit, Defined 312
Profits, Discussed 33, 35-36, 47, 48, 52, 53, 55, 61, 64, 73, 76-77, 79, 81, 132, 151, 154, 162, 166, 168, 172, 185, 186, 191, 193, 194, 195-199, 213, 215-216, 221-222, 238, 241-242, 247, 248-249, 250, 251
Promoting Products 119-122
Property Tax 279
Public Offering 145, 146, 154, 158, 159-161, 312

Realism 12, 21-22
Reebok Shoes 97
Resale Tax Number 279
Reserving a Corporate Name 268
Resources 297-301
Respect for Others 208-209
Retail Businesses 44-57
Retained Earnings 312
Rewards 255-257
Risk-Taking 24-26, 53-54

"S" Corporation 269, 281
Safeway Stores 105
Sales
    Compared with Marketing 183-185
    Compensation 197-199
    General 183-202
    Strategy 184-185
Sales and Use Tax 278
Sales Representatives 184, 188, 190, 191, 194, 198, 199, 227
Sales Slumps 199-201
Scotchgard 17
Second-Round Financing 145, 146, 312-313
Secured Loan 141, 313
Securities and Exchange Commission 83, 299
Securities Laws 84, 129, 288-289
Security, Defined 313

Seed Capital 145, 146, 147, 313
Selecting a Business Idea 33-69
Self-Confidence 206
Self-Understanding 211
Service Businesses 44-57
Signet 108
Simplicity 15-16, 77-79, 212-213
Sliding-Scale Valuation 168, 170-172
Slinky 17
Slogans
    Importance 102-103
    Protecting 108-109, 268-269, 286
Small Business Administration 52,
    78, 164, 266, 269, 297, 298
Social Security 273, 278, 299
Sole Proprietorship 269-270
Standard Brands 105
Start-Up Capital 313
Start-Up Financing 129, 145, 146
Stockholders' Agreement 281-282
Success 237-246
    Measures
        Business Plan Goals 245
        Cash Reserves 240
        Entrepreneur's Goals 245-
        246
        Industry Comparisons 240
        Profits 241-242
        Response of Financiers 242-
        245
        Sales Base 240-241

Target Market 92-97
Taxes
    Business Transfer 279-280
    Income 279
    Payroll 277-278
    Property 279
    Sales and Use 278
    Social Security 279
    State Income 279
Teamwork 209-210
Telemarketing 187, 292
Temptations 248-255
Test Marketing 97, 122
Thomson and Thomson 268
3M Corporation 17, 38
Toys-R-Us 103, 104

Trade Associations 52, 78, 148, 165,
    301
Trade Names 301
Trade Secrets 281, 285, 288
Trademarks 108-109, 267-268, 269,
    285-286
Turbo Pascal 104

Unemployment Insurance 273, 278
Union Oil 105
Universal Product Code ("UPC") 276
Unsecured Loan 141, 153, 313

Venture Capital 155-158, 313-314
Venture Capital Clubs 148
Venture Capitalist 154, 155-158, 314

Warrant 141, 154, 314
Westin 108
Wholesalers 188, 189
WordPerfect 104
Workers' Compensation Insurance
    273, 275, 290
Working Capital 146, 153, 314

Xerox Technology 26

*Thank you for your interest in*
# The Entrepreneur's Road Map!

CO-AUTHORS
## LYLE MAUL AND DIANNE MAYFIELD

**are pleased to announce
the formation of**

## VENTURE SERVICES GROUP[SM]
*– a consulting firm*
**Committed to Helping Businesses Grow**

Lyle and Dianne have assembled a team of skilled professionals who can help create and grow businesses. With offices on the East and West Coasts, the Venture Services Group ("VSG") offers a full range of business consulting services. If you are interested in learning more about VSG's services, or if you wish to approach the authors concerning speaking engagements, you may contact the **VENTURE SERVICES GROUP** at either of its offices:

**West Coast Office**
Attn: Lyle Maul
3420 Ocean Park Blvd.
Suite 2000
Santa Monica, CA 90405
(213) 392-3395

**East Coast Office**
Attn: Dianne Mayfield
P.O. Box 1609
Alexandria, VA 22313

(703) 836-9290